enjoying
COMBAT
SPORTS

enjoying COMBAT SPORTS

by the Diagram Group

Stoeger Publishing Company

Copyright © 1977 Diagram Visual Information Ltd.

Published by Stoeger Publishing Company
55 Ruta Court
South Hackensack, New Jersey 07606

Second printing, August 1981

Distributed to the book trade and to the sporting goods trade
by Stoeger Industries, 55 Ruta Court, South Hackensack,
New Jersey 07606

In Canada, distributed to the book trade and to the sporting
goods trade by Stoeger Canada, Ltd., 165 Idema Road,
Markham, Ontario L3R 1A9

Printed and bound in the United States of America

ISBN 0-88317-099-X

Foreword

There is a story of how Richard the Lion Heart, the crusader king of England, tried to impress his enemy, the Moslem Saladin, by chopping an anvil in half with his two-handed sword. Saladin respectfully replied by slicing a silk cushion into pieces with his scimitar. The story reveals the essence of the martial arts. One hero demonstrates strength, the other skill. A wise person tries to combine both.

This book is about competitive combat sports, practiced to agreed rules, under the watchful eye of a judge or referee. They are not a training in aggression, or a preparation for attacking people. None of the actions or exercises described within has the purpose of hurting or disabling someone. The sports are ones that an enthusiast may see on TV, watch in the stadium, or practice in a gymnasium.

Enjoying Combat Sports has two main sections: unarmed combat, and armed. These are divided in turn into sports that originated in the western world, and those that started in the East but are now popular in the West as well. The origins and main features of each sport are described, together with its official rules, and in each case there are also ideas for simple training techniques and a glossary of special terms used.

These often complex sports are explained throughout by a special combination of illustration and clear, precise text. The editors and illustrators hope that this will make combat sports easier for the reader to understand – and enjoy.

Contents

Boxing

Boxing in a saloon in 19th-century Australia. The skills of the boxing ring have always appealed to the self-reliant.

Unarmed combat between individuals is as old as man himself. In fact, many people believe that such combat is quite natural: that certain individuals will always respond to the challenge of another person's strength, and feel the need to prove themselves stronger and more agile.

Over many centuries, the rules and customs of such fights gradually established themselves. Contests became tests of a combatant's strength and skill, both mental and physical, in outwitting his opponent, rather than displays of mere brute force. This is not to deny the fact that a fighter may get hurt, often painfully, sometimes badly – that is a risk which anyone who practices a combat sport has to accept. The point is that contestants do not set out deliberately to maim one another.

Before the Queensberry Rules were introduced in 1865, most boxers fought with their bare hands, often in prize rings at fairs and country shows. These contests tested endurance, not skill, and were little more than glorified punching matches.

Today, boxers must command speed and precision in both attack and defense. Training is long and hard, but the rewards can be great.

Both kicking and punching are allowed in Thai kick boxing, in contrast to boxing in Europe and the Americas. This national sport is full of traditions. Before the fight, contestants dance around the ring, staring at the audience in an attempt to ward off evil spirits. Women are also thought to bring bad luck.

There are many different forms of the ancient sport of wrestling. In the West the two most popular are Greco-Roman (in which only the body above the waist is used) and freestyle. In each case, the aim is to pin both an opponent's shoulders to the mat. (The wrestling usually seen on television is an entertainment, not a sport.)

Sumo is a variety of wrestling practiced in Japan by men weighing at least 350 pounds. Although the contests contain much ceremony, the object is the same — to pin an opponent helpless to the ground. Another national form is Yagli, from Turkey. The contestants cover their bodies with grease, making holds especially difficult.

Among the most popular oriental martial sports are judo, in which the aim is to throw one's opponent; karate, which is built around the striking power of the hands and feet; and aikido, which matches force with avoiding action. "Kung-fu" is a Chinese form of karate.

Boxing

Boxing as we know it today – a fast, scientific sport for gloved fighters – dates from the formulation of the Queensberry Rules in 1865. These were set down by the Marquis of Queensberry and, though they have been much modified, still remain the basis of the sport.

In 1865, the days of the prize ring were nearly over, and gloved fighting was becoming increasingly popular. Fights in the prize ring (which first developed in the early 18th century) were tests of endurance rather than skill and lasted for a large number of rounds (on one occasion as many as 42!)

Once gloves began to be worn, techniques inevitably changed. Since it was now much easier to knock out an opponent – simply because bare hands were weaker and could give less punishment – defense became more important. Boxers had to use their feet to move out of the range of an opponent's blows and as part of overall tactics.

The mental and physical agility, rather than mere slogging strength, that are required of a successful boxer today are the direct result of the Queensberry Rules. What the boxer also encounters today, which he did not a century ago, is the whole business of modern stardom: exposure to the press and television, large sums in prize money, and relentless pressure to succeed.

Early boxers rose to fame on their mere physical endurance.

THE SECOND CONTEST BETWEEN CRIB & MOLINEUX, SEPT.ᵣ 28ᵗʰ 1811.

Published by Geo: Smeeton, Decᵣ 17, 1812.

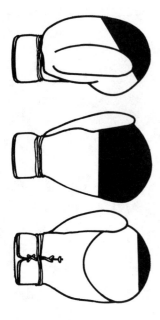

If you want to see whether you will enjoy boxing or are any good at it, get your gym teacher at school or at a youth club to give you some lessons. But you won't become a boxer overnight: as in all sports, training is the watchword. Some of the basic principles of boxing are illustrated on the next few pages. Study them, put in hours of disciplined training (see pp. 30–32), and you might just have a chance of success!

In most countries, amateur contests are the usual starting-point for a boxer. The controlling organizations – such as the Amateur Athletic Union in the United States and the Amateur Boxing Association in Great Britain – select teams for international matches and for the Olympics, and also organize a wide range of national contests. So a first bout in a school or town competition might eventually lead, for those with both talent and dedication, to membership of a national team.

You win at boxing by knocking out your opponent, or by scoring more points than he does. But not all punches score points. To score, a punch must use the "knuckle" area of the glove (above), and must land on the target area of your opponent – that is, the front and sides of his head and his body above the belt (right).

Some parts of your target are rather vulnerable to blows (**a**): the chin, heart, and solar plexus, for example. But your opponent will do his best to keep these well guarded (**b**). Most punches outside the target area simply do not score. But some are actually illegal, such as ones on the back of the neck, over the kidneys (**c**), and below the belt.

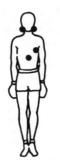
a

b

c

The key to success in boxing is to hit hard, hit quickly, and move quickly. More fights are won with the feet than with the hands. While a fighter must of course be able to punch well, it is even more vital to keep out of an opponent's reach – and then suddenly dart in with an unexpected blow.

Boxing is also a matter of tactics. Different boxers have different styles, and a fighter must judge the best way of dealing with an opponent. A tall fighter, for example, may have the advantages of reach and strength. But he is often too slow-moving to defend himself well at close quarters.

Advice on tactics is one of the jobs of a boxer's "seconds". Each boxer is allowed a set number of these helpers, who escort him to the ring. At least one of them is allowed to attend him in the ring between rounds, giving advice and encouragement and attending to any injuries.

If you do take up boxing, always remember it is not a free-for-all. Never hit an opponent when he is down – that is, if any part of his body apart from his feet is touching the ground (or if he is lying helpless through or on the ropes). Retire to the further neutral corner, and wait until the referee orders the fight to continue.

Outfighting – that is, long-range work – is the most important technique a boxer has to master. The more skillful a boxer is, the less he fights close in to his opponent, and the more he relies on long blows and rapid movement. On this page and the next are shown the basics of long-distance attack.

basic stance

To take up guard in the basic boxing stance, stand with legs apart, left foot forward, and body turned sideways to your opponent. Your right heel should be slightly raised, and the right leg flexed, but keep your weight evenly on both feet. Tuck your elbows close in to your body, and hold the left glove out at shoulder height, loosely clenched, with thumb uppermost. Hold your right glove underneath your chin, halfway between open and clenched, with wrist toward you and knuckles toward your opponent.

footwork

Good footwork is vital: be light on your feet, but be steady on them too. For good balance, keep the feet apart when you move. As the diagram shows, the foot to move first is the one nearer the direction you want to go. So if you are moving right, for example, glide the right foot out first, to widen your base; then bring the left one after it.

punching

A really effective punch needs the body's weight behind it. Imagine that you are trying to punch through the target. On a straight punch, the fist should twist so the back of the hand is turned up on impact.

straight left

More than any other punch, this forces an opponent to keep his distance. Simply straighten your left arm, turning hips and shoulders into the blow. The fist will twist to knuckles up just before impact. If you have room, slide your left foot forward for the blow; but bring the right up at once to regain balance.

left hook

This is a bent-arm blow, used at close quarters. From the basic stance, twist violently to the right at the hips and shoulders, taking your weight onto your right foot. The left arm hooks sideways, wrist bent, and the fist is driven into the side of your opponent's head or body.

uppercuts

These are upward blows to the chin or body, with the elbow bent. The right-hand one is the more useful. From the basic stance, take your weight onto your right foot, leaning slightly that way. Then, from shoulders and hips, twist hard to the left, driving off from your right foot, and jerking your right forearm up into your target.

straight right

This is powered by a sudden twist from the waist, jerking the left shoulder back and driving the right arm straight forward. If there is room, you can also drive the body's weight forward onto the left foot. The punch is very powerful, but tiring if you miss – and it may leave you wide open to counterattack.

Successful infighting – when boxers fight close up to one another – demands more sheer strength and less calculation and skill than outfighting. Nevertheless it forms an important part of every match.

getting to close quarters
You can usually do this by parrying or sidestepping (**a**) your opponent's left lead. But do not rush in blindly. Crouch slightly, with elbows well tucked in and guard up. You need to keep both your opponent's arms outside your own (**b**).

punches
Use short hooks (**a**) and uppercuts (**b**) to the body and chin. Vary these: a sudden uppercut to the chin may make your opponent raise his guard, leaving his body exposed.

breaking away
This can be tricky. One way (**a**) is to put your gloves on your opponent's arms and give yourself a sharp push back with your guard well up. Another (**b**) is to let his weight carry him forward as you sidestep, turning him with your right hand and then pushing off with your left.

clinch and break
During infighting, arms often get tangled, so no one can hit properly. This is called a clinch (**a**), and the referee will tell you to "break." You must then step back a pace from each other before you carry on. It is a foul (**b**) to hit your opponent on the break.

Defense needs practice, as well as attack. Good defense demands skill and quick reflexes. Only in the last resort should a boxer have to "cover up" until the fury of an attack is spent.

To defend yourself from a punch you can:
a sidestep
b "snap back"
c sway to one side
d take the punch on your forearm, shoulder, or elbow
e stop it with your glove
f duck beneath it
g parry it to one side
h cover up.

It is not enough to avoid your opponent's punches. You must come straight back onto counterattack, or he will simply try again. The diagrams on this page all show counters to the straight left, for this is the punch you will have to face most often. But with other punches the same principles apply.

straight left counters
a Block your opponent's left with your glove, and return a left jab to his chin.
b Duck beneath your opponent's left, and return a straight left to his body.

straight right counters
a Duck inside your opponent's left, so it passes over your right shoulder. Then throw a straight right back to his head, over his arm. Twist from the hips to get your weight into it.
b Slide left and throw a straight right back inside your opponent's left jab.

other counters
a Parry your opponent's left over your left shoulder. Then pivot sharply to your right, to throw a left hook to his chin.
b Slide to the right and slip outside your opponent's left. Then twist back to the left to uppercut with a right to his body. (Follow this up with a left hook if possible.)

A southpaw is a boxer whose normal stance is with the right arm extended – in other words, a mirror image of the normal. It is worth learning how to deal with such a fighter, for while the conventional boxer rarely meets a southpaw, southpaws are accustomed to fighting conventional boxers – and so have an advantage over them. The basic rules are never move to your right, against a southpaw, or drop your left-hand guard. If you do, you will be exposed to his strong left hand. In these diagrams, as usual, you are the boxer in black.

southpaw tactics
a You try a straight left. The southpaw sidesteps left, and sends a straight right back to your chin.
b You try a straight left. The southpaw ducks under it, sways right, and gets in a left to your body.

counter tactics
The southpaw tries a straight right.
a You parry it, and counter with a straight right to the chin.
b You slip inside it, and hook a left back over his arm.
c You duck under it, and follow this with
d a right to his body.

Boxing can be practiced from
an early age, for its skills are
basic ones, founded on quick
reactions and physical agility.

Rules of boxing

Boxing is a tightly controlled sport. Rules on every aspect of the conduct of contests are laid down by the various national and international associations.

the ring
Most contests are held in a three-roped ring, though in amateur bouts two ropes are also allowed. The floor must be of canvas, with an underlay of felt or rubber. A ring may be no bigger than 20 feet square or smaller than 14 feet square (12 feet square for an amateur contest). The floor of the ring must extend for at least $1\frac{1}{2}$ feet beyond the ropes.

officials
For both amateur and professional fights, the officials consist of:
a the referee
b judges, who score the contest
c the timekeeper
d official seconds (each boxer is permitted two seconds, and in professional contests up to four may be allowed).

the referee
The referee has complete control over what takes place within the ring. In particular he looks after the boxers; administers cautions for rule-breaking; controls the corners (for example, he sees that only those permitted to do so attend the boxers); gives the count; and stops the contest if necessary.
In addition, the referee may act as one of the three judges (except in professional contests in Great Britain, where there are no separate judges, and the referee alone decides the result).

dress

Amateur boxers wear shorts and undershirts, professionals shorts only.

equipment

Essential equipment for both amateur and professional boxers includes gloves, gumshield, binding tape, and lightweight boxing boots.

gloves

Eight-ounce gloves are the usual ones for both amateur and professional boxers. But six-ounce gloves are worn by professional fighters at welterweight level and below, and by some amateur juniors, while in some countries 10-ounce gloves are used by heavyweights.

bandage

To protect their hands, amateurs may use up to 8 feet 4 inches of $1\frac{3}{4}$-inch-wide soft dry bandage, or 6 feet 6 inches of $1\frac{3}{4}$-inch-wide

Velpeau dry bandage, on each hand. Professionals are permitted up to 18 feet of 2-inch-wide soft dry bandage, and/or 11 feet of 1-inch-wide zinc oxide tape (9 feet at middleweight or below). Tape may not be wound over the knuckles.

weigh in

At the weigh in, on the day of the fight, fight officials ensure that the contestants are not over- or underweight for their class, and also give them a thorough medical examination.

Official weight limits	AIBA	WBC	EBU	BBB of C
Light flyweight	48 kg	108 lb	—	—
Flyweight	51	112	112	112
Bantamweight	54	118	118	118
Super bantamweight	—	122	—	—
Featherweight	57	126	126	126
Junior lightweight	—	130	130[1]	—
Lightweight	60	135	135	135
Light welterweight	63·5	140[2]	140[3]	140
Welterweight	67	147	147	147
Light middleweight	71	154	154[4]	154
Middleweight	75	160	160	160
Light heavyweight	81	175	175	175
Heavyweight	over 81	over 175	over 175	any weight

AIBA (Amateur International Boxing Association) weights apply to all amateur boxing contests. **WBC** (World Boxing Council) weights apply to all professional world championships, **EBU** (European Boxing Union) weights to all professional European championships, **BBB of C** (British Boxing Board of Control) weights to all professional contests in Great Britain.

[1] termed Super featherweight.
[2] termed Junior welterweight.
[3] termed Super lightweight.
[4] termed Super welterweight.

the bout

Once the boxers are in their corners and ready to fight, they are called to the center of the ring. The referee asks if they understand the rules of the fight. Then they shake hands and the bout begins. It is divided into anything from three to 15 rounds (depending on the type of contest) of two or three minutes each. There is a one-minute break after each round, during which the fighters return to their corners and are attended by their seconds. Start and finish of each round are signaled by the timekeeper's bell.

the result

A bout can be won:
on points, after the full number of rounds;
by a count-out, when one boxer is knocked down for a count of 10 seconds;
by one of the contestants being disqualified;
or by one of the contestants being declared unfit to continue (either by the referee or by his own seconds).

the count

When a contestant is knocked down, the referee orders the standing boxer to go to a neutral corner, and then takes up the count to 10 from the timekeeper. If the boxer does not rise by the count of 10, he loses the contest (even – in professional boxing – if the end of a round is reached during the count). If he rises before 10, the fight goes on. (In amateur bouts, and some professional ones, the count always goes to eight, before the boxers may "box on.")

points decision

In amateur boxing, the boxers are awarded points during the contest for the number of scoring blows that they land (see p. 14). The boxer with the larger number of scoring blows in a round gains a set number of points for that round (usually 20). The other boxer receives points in proportion to the number of blows he scored. If the bout ends without a count-out, disqualification, etc., these points are totaled to decide which boxer has won. There are no draws in amateur boxing. If scores are equal at the end of a bout, the boxer who attacked more wins. If the bout is still undecided, the boxer with the better style wins. If the bout remains unresolved, victory goes to the boxer with the better defense.

Similar principles apply in professional boxing, but points are awarded for attack, defense, initiative, and style, rather than just for scoring blows. In most countries the maximum number of points for a round is 10. If scores are equal at the end of the contest, a draw is declared.

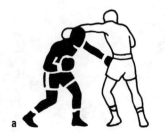
a

b

d

e

g

h

c

f

i

fouls

It is illegal to land a punch on certain areas outside the target: eg, below the belt (**a**), on the back of the neck (**b**), and over the kidneys (**c**). Pivot or backhanded blows also count as fouls, as do blows with the butt of the hand (**d**), the wrist, or the elbow (**e**). Also, boxers may not deliberately strike their opponent with the inside of the glove (**f**).

Some body contact is also illegal – such as butting (**g**), careless use of the head, shouldering the opponent, or wrestling with him.

Other fouls include: persistently ducking below the waistline (**h**); failing to step back from a clinch when ordered to "break"; deliberately punching an opponent while he is falling or when he is on the floor (**i**); holding onto the ropes with one or both hands, whether for attack or for defense; and not trying to win.

The referee may also rule as a foul any act that he considers to be outside the rules.

Fouls are punished by a warning, which brings with it a loss of points. Persistent misconduct leads to disqualification.

A boxer, whether he is a professional or an ambitious amateur, must be prepared to lead a tough, austere life. Regular, vigorous training, a strict diet, and early nights and plenty of sleep, are just some of the things that will separate his life-style from that of his friends and contemporaries. Taken seriously, boxing demands almost total dedication.

On this page and the next are shown some of the training exercises and equipment most often used. Even if you only fight from time to time at school or in your local club, you will find them useful.

Roadwork (perhaps as much as a five-mile run every day) is an essential part of training.

Most of a boxer's training takes place in the gym, where a sweat suit is worn. Jogging on the spot toughens the leg muscles, push-ups the arm muscles. Work with a jumping rope aids footwork and balance and helps to build up stamina. The "on the spot" bikes and rowing machines available in most gyms help to maintain overall fitness.

Shadow-boxing – that is, fighting an imaginary opponent – helps to develop the reflexes and encourages quick thinking.

Punching strength is best developed on a punchbag – a suspended canvas or leather sack usually filled with sand or sawdust. The punchball – an inflated ball attached to a spring – helps to coordinate hand and eye and to perfect timing and speed.

Weights and chest-expanders help to toughen arm and chest muscles and to ensure overall strength and fitness.

One of the most effective ways of obtaining general fighting experience and working for a particular contest is to train with a sparring partner. He should be as like the prospective opponent in style and build as possible.

Sparring is not fighting. The aim is not to defeat an opponent but to practice the various boxing skills and to reach fighting pitch.

By sparring, you start learning to cope with different boxing styles. Some opponents rush in, others try to tempt you to attack; some jab persistently from a distance, others want to draw you into infighting.

Headguards, foul protectors, and specially padded gloves, are normally worn during sparring to prevent injury.

When sparring, make sure that you learn how to dominate the ring. Keep to the center, and make your partner move about as much as possible. Then, in an actual contest, you will probably be able to make your opponent move faster than he normally does – so robbing him of his wind, strength, and punching power, and of his resistance to your punches.

Break	Referee's command to boxers to withdraw from clinch.
Butting	Illegal use of head to hit opponent.
Clinch	Position in which the contestants' arms become intertwined.
Count	Count by referee from 1 to 10 that takes place when boxer has been knocked to the floor of the ring or is lying through or helpless on the ropes.
Count-out	Defeat of boxer through his failure to rise by the count of 10.
Counter	Punch made after successful avoidance of an opponent's punch.
Foul protector	Guard worn by boxers around groin during sparring practice.
Guard	Defensive position adopted by boxers to shield themselves from an opponent's blows.
Gumshield	Piece of plastic clenched in the mouth during a fight to protect the teeth and prevent the tongue being bitten.
Headguard	Head protector used by boxers during sparring practice.
Hook	Sideways blow delivered (by either hand) with elbow in hooked position.
Infighting	Those parts of a bout during which contestants fight close up to one another.
Jab	Quick punch that does not have the boxer's full weight behind it.
Knock-out blow	Blow that knocks a boxer unconscious.
Outfighting	Those parts of a bout during which the contestants remain at arm's length from one another.

Parry	Deflection of an opponent's punch with glove or arm.
Points	Score given to a boxer for his performance during a fight. Used to decide the result if the bout ends without a count-out, disqualification, etc.
Queensberry Rules	The first official rules of boxing, laid down by the Marquis of Queensberry in 1865.
Round	A fighting period, lasting two or three minutes. Any bout is divided into a number of these, with one-minute rest intervals in between.
Second	Attendant who escorts boxer to ring and advises and tends him between rounds.
Shadow-boxing	Training technique in which the boxer practices on his own.
Southpaw	Left-handed boxer.
Slip	Sideways movement to avoid a punch.
Snap back	Sudden swaying of body backward, to avoid a punch.
Sparring	Training sessions or fights with a partner.
Straight left	Blow delivered with left fist, arm outstretched.
Straight right	Blow delivered with right fist, arm outstretched.
Thai kick boxing	Form of boxing from Thailand, in which both punching and kicking are permitted.
Uppercut	Upward-moving blow (from either hand) delivered with the larger knuckles.
Weigh in	Ceremony at which contestants are weighed, to ensure that they are within the limits for their division (see p. 25).

Wrestling

A 19th-century engraving of a wrestling scene in the Swiss countryside. Wrestling was always a popular trial of strength wherever rural communities gathered for games and festivities.

Wrestling

That wrestling is one of the oldest of sports is not surprising. Its basic techniques are central to successful self-defense, and it was natural that they be tested in competition. Wrestling was practiced in ancient China and Egypt, and was also popular at the Greek Olympic Games. There, and later in Roman times, one of the main styles still used today, the Greco-Roman, was developed. In more modern times, the popularity of wrestling really soared in the 18th century, when watching fights in the prize ring became a standard pastime.

Gradually, as the 19th century drew on, wrestling was overshadowed by boxing. To attract back the crowds, professional wrestlers became more and more showmen rather than sportsmen. But the formation of the International Wrestling Federation in 1912 ensured the survival of amateur wrestling, and today the distinction between the amateur and professional forms of the sport is very clear. Professional wrestlers, especially when they appear on television, are entertainers who aim to please their fans – though this is not to doubt their skill. By contrast, amateur wrestling is conducted to a strict set of rules, and it is amateur wrestling that is discussed in the following pages.

Wrestling is an all-round sport in which no one part of the body is developed at the expense of another. It also demands considerable mental alertness. Practiced correctly, it is very safe. Serious injuries are rare, although of course a wrestler must be prepared to put up with occasional bruises and strains. Indeed, on the whole wrestlers keep on fighting for much longer than any other sportsmen – one famous wrestler continued to appear in the ring until he was 65!

Wrestling is the simplest to
set up of all combat contests,
and its popularity is universal.

When this statue of Greek
wrestlers was made, the sport
was already thousands of
years old.

Amateur wrestlers normally meet on a mat, rather than in a ring. But of course a contest could be held on any smooth surface, such as grass, from which all sharp objects have been removed.

The basic aim in a contest is to force the opponent to the ground, and to hold his shoulders to the mat.

In their attempts to pin each other to the mat, wrestlers grapple with each other, using a variety of holds.

Understanding the principles of leverage – and using them – is essential for success in wrestling. Most techniques depend on levering an opponent into an awkward position, rather than on mere brute force.

One major international style of amateur wrestling is freestyle (which used to be known more frequently as catch-as-catch-can). Contestants in freestyle bouts may use the whole of their bodies, including the legs. But this does not mean it is a free-for-all. In fact, body contact between contestants is very carefully controlled (see p. 54).

Greco-Roman is the other main style of amateur wrestling at the international level. In Greco-Roman contests, wrestlers are only allowed to fight each other with their arms and upper parts of their bodies. All leg holds and movements – such as tripping – are forbidden.

Other old wrestling styles are not dying out. One such is Cumberland and Westmorland, a traditional style from the north of England and Scotland. In this, contestants clasp their arms behind each other's backs, and must remain in this hold throughout the bout.

Collegiate and high school amateur wrestling are forms practiced by students in the U.S.A. and Canada. They are nearly identical to international freestyle. Professional wrestling (far right) is concerned with showmanship, not competition, and uses many techniques forbidden to amateurs.

After a fight has begun, a contestant's first aim is to force his opponent to the ground. This is known as the takedown, and on this page and the next some of the most commonly used takedowns are shown. Note that the techniques on this and following pages are for the beginner at freestyle (or collegiate) wrestling. If an amateur does develop an interest in the Greco-Roman style, it is usually only after some years of freestyle experience. Also note that directions such as "left" and "right" tie in with the diagrams — but you can easily reverse them, to attack from the other side.

starting

The bout opens with the contestants in the sparring position. This is a very important moment. A good wrestler must be able to sum up his opponent quickly, and decide how he will set about taking him down.

arm drag

This is one takedown from the sparring position. Grab your opponent's right elbow and spin him around in front of you (**1**), at the same time going down onto one knee and grasping his right ankle. Then, with one arm around his waist and your head in front of his leg (**2**), you lever him down.

1   **2**

pull-by

For this, grip your opponent's arm (**1**). and pull him toward you as you turn (**2**). Then drag him toward the mat with your right arm (**3**), at the same time grasping his leg behind the thigh with your left arm (**4**). Now swing him round so you are on top of him, with one leg hooked over his (**5**).

1   **2**

1 2 3

drag and trip (above)
This is a takedown from the common standing tie-up shown (**1**). Roll your opponent's right arm down, thus releasing his grip on your elbow, and catch it with your right hand, while stepping in and pulling him back (**2**). At the same time trip your right leg behind his. Push him back over your right leg, pressing your right arm against his chest (**3**).

single leg dive (below)
Begin by making a dive for your opponent's right leg (**1**). Circle to his right, grabbing his heel with your right hand (**2**). Now stand up suddenly – placing your left arm and shoulder around your opponent's waist, and keeping your head outside his right knee – and trip him to the floor (**3**).

1 2 3

3 4 5

Once a contestant has successfully taken down his opponent, the next stage is to try to break him down – that is, to force him onto his stomach or his side. On this page and the next are shown some of the more common breakdowns.

referee's position

The official starting position on the ground (**1**) is known as the referee's position (see p.54). The defending wrestler kneels with knees slightly apart and hands firmly on the floor at shoulder width, palms down and fingers stretched out. This is the strongest stance a wrestler can adopt once he has been taken down to the mat. The other wrestler will often begin his attack by grasping one of the defending wrestler's arms (**2**).

bar arm and waistlock

This is a commonly used breakdown. Pull your opponent's near arm out (**1**), grasping him firmly around the waist with your other arm at the same time. This will cause him to fall onto the mat; then keep him pinned there (**2**).

hip breakdown

This is another effective breakdown. Push your left knee against your opponent's right knee (**1**), keeping your left arm around his waist and your right on his elbow. Now use your arms and knee to lever him onto the mat (**2**).

1

2

3

cross-body ride

One of the most difficult of breakdowns. From the referee's position (**1**), climb onto your opponent's right leg, keeping your right arm on his elbow, and your left arm around his waist (**2**). Then straighten out and force his right leg to the right, inserting your own right leg in front of his (**3**). Now move across his body (**4**) and encircle his left arm (**5**), so forcing him onto the mat.

4

5

far ankle and far arm

From the starting position (**1**), suddenly release your opponent's near arm, and grasp his far arm just above the elbow (**2**). Pull his arm under his chest and grab his ankle with your other hand (**3**). That will send him onto the mat and enable you to pin him down on his far ankle, far arm, and chest (**4**).

1

2

3

4

All the pinning techniques shown here can bring a successful fall: that is, when the attacking wrestler holds both his opponent's shoulders to the mat and so wins the bout.

bar arm and half nelson

This can follow a bar arm and waistlock breakdown. Start by stepping over your opponent's right leg with your left knee (**1**), thus forcing him forward, at the same time thrusting his right arm under his body so you can grip his wrist with both hands (**2**). Now move to the left, forcing his head down with your left arm and thrusting your right arm under his body (**3**).Pull his head down and move to the left driving him onto his shoulders (**4**). Finally pin him to the mat by moving right over him (**5**).

reverse half nelson

Used after the cross-body ride. From the cross-body position (**1**), grab your opponent's left arm, and lift it over your head (**2**). Now lie back (**3**), and so lever his shoulders onto the mat (**4**). Lock your hands together for the fall (**5**).

shoulder roll

Used after a bar arm and waistlock breakdown. Press your inside knee into your opponent's thigh, at the same time buckling his near arm under (**1**). Then, locking your hands around him, pull him toward your hip (**2**), so sending him onto his shoulders (**3**). Then throw your legs across his head (**4**), thus pinning him tight.

lace-ride combination

This can be used after a successful hip breakdown. First lace your left arm between your opponent's legs (**1**), and then pull up one of his legs. This will force him onto the mat, and you can hold him there in what is known as a cradle-fall hold (**2**).

Of course, wrestling bouts are not one-sided. A good wrestler knows how to escape from each of the various takedown, breakdown, and pinning techniques. Some of these countering methods are described on this page and the next.

1

2

3

takedown counters

To deal with a pull-by takedown (above), grasp the top of the attacking wrestler's right arm, and drop your weight to the right (**1**). You now have leverage to pull him past you (**2**) to the mat (**3**). (The counter to the drag and trip is very similar, but you need to grasp the opponent's thigh with your free hand, to help bring him past you.)

To counter the single-leg dive, simply lift your leg as the opponent tackles it, and flatten yourself out (right) on top of your opponent, pressing down on his shoulders.

1

2

3

breakdown counters

A good way of resisting the bar arm and waistlock breakdown is the swimmer's break (above). Starting from the tie-up position, you roll onto your right side (**1**), thread your left arm over your opponent's (**2**), and grasp his wrist. Now you can lever off his grip, leaving your right hand free (**3**).

To counter the far arm and ankle breakdown, you prevent your opponent gripping your far arm by moving it quickly away (right).

referee's position counter
If you are defending in the referee's position (**1**), one escape is as follows. Pivot on your knee (**2**), and with your right foot step into a sitting position, but raised off the mat (**3**). Grip your opponent's inside thigh with your left hand, and lean back so that you are pressing on his left shoulder (**4**). Continue to lean back, and reach for his buttocks with your left hand (**5**), at the same time turning toward him and stepping back with your left foot (**6**).

pinning counters
The reverse half nelson can be countered (above) by sliding your left arm away (**1**), and rolling your opponent over your hips (**2**). Then you can pull your arm free (**3**).

To counter the shoulder roll, straighten out as your opponent tries to turn you, so you are in a prone position on the mat (right). This makes it difficult for him to roll you over and pin you down.

Rules of wrestling

The following pages set out the international rules covering both main modern styles of amateur wrestling: freestyle and Greco-Roman.

the mat

The contest area is a circle 9 meters in diameter. It consists of the central wrestling surface, colored yellow, which is a circle 7 meters in diameter; and a 1-meter wide border outside this, colored red, called the passivity zone. The center of the contest area is marked by a white circle. Beyond the passivity zone, outside the contest area, is a further border, colored blue, called the protection surface.

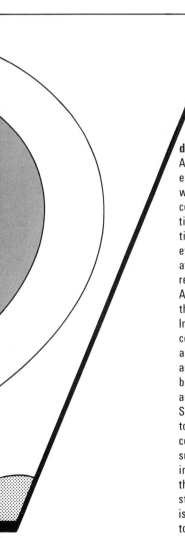

duration

A bout lasts for three rounds, each of three minutes actual wrestling time, unless one competitor wins before the time limit (see p. 53). The timekeeper announces the time every minute, and rings the bell at the end of each round. The referee then blows his whistle. Actions between the bell and the whistle are invalid.
In the 1-minute intervals each contestant may be instructed and attended by his masseur and trainer until five seconds before the bell is rung to announce the next round. Should either contestant have to halt for reasons beyond his control, the referee must suspend the bout. If the interruption lasts for more than five minutes, the bout stops altogether. (Five minutes is the total injury time allowed to a wrestler in a tournament.)

officials

At every contest the following officials must be present:
a mat chairman
b referee
c judge
d timekeeper.

mat chairman

The mat chairman is the chief official. He supervises the work of the other officials, and decides in any disagreement between them.

referee

The referee must be dressed in white, with a red sleeve on one arm, and a blue one on the other. His duties are:
to start, interrupt, and end bouts;
to inspect the wrestlers at the start of each round;
to warn or caution them if necessary;
to indicate the points they score, the validity of holds, whether they are in the contest area, when either of them has been placed in danger (see p. 52), and when a fall has occurred.

judge

The judge marks the score sheet, on the basis of his own observations and the referee's signals. If he disagrees with the referee, the mat chairman makes the final decision. The judge announces the winner if there is no fall.

weight categories

As in boxing, wrestlers only meet others in their weight category. The category limits are 48kg, 52, 57, 62, 68, 74, 82, 90, 100, and 100 or over.

dress

Contestants must wear a tight-fitting one-piece costume (**a**) in red or blue, and either a jockstrap or a support belt. They must also carry a handkerchief. Light knee-guards are allowed; bandages are not unless prescribed by a doctor. Shoes must not have heels, nailed soles, metal parts, or buckles. Contestants are forbidden to cover their skins with oil or grease and must be clean shaven, unless their beards are · several months old. Fingernails must be cut short.

a

start of bout

At the start of the bout the wrestlers shake hands in the center of the mat, are inspected by the referee, and then return to their corners to wait until the referee starts the bout. Contestants start each round in a standing position (**b**).

b

wrestling on the ground

The bout continues even if one wrestler has been brought to the ground. If he is able to, the wrestler underneath may counter his opponent's efforts and get up.

A wrestler who brings his opponent to the ground must be active. If both wrestlers are passive, they must resume in the standing position.

c

placing in danger

A wrestler is said to be placed in danger (of a fall) when, with his back to the mat, he is in a position more than 90 degrees away from the vertical, while resisting with the upper part of his body. Examples are when a wrestler:

forms a bridge to avoid a fall (**c**);

rests on his elbows to keep his shoulders off the mat;

lies on one shoulder with the other shoulder more than 90 degrees away from vertical;

or touches the mat with both shoulders for less than a second.

If a wrestler goes into an in danger position (however briefly), points are awarded to his opponent (see p. 53).

the fall

For a fall to be registered, both the wrestler's shoulders must remain in contact with the mat (**d**) long enough for the referee to count one or say to himself "tomber" (fall). The referee signals the fall by striking the mat with his hand and blowing his whistle.

d

winning

A wrestler can win:
by scoring a fall;
by leading on points at the end of nine minutes;
or by his opponent being eliminated after three cautions, or disqualified, or retiring through injury.

scoring a bout

Points are scored for a "major technical hold." This is one that makes the opponent lose all contact with the ground, controls him tightly, takes him through a broad sweeping curve in space, and brings him to the ground in a direct and immediate position of danger. Three points are awarded for the hold, and one additional point if the position of danger is held for five seconds or more. Points are also scored in other ways. One point is scored for:
bringing an opponent to the mat and holding him down in control;
moving from the underneath to the uppermost position in control;
applying a correct hold without causing an opponent to touch the mat with his head or shoulders;
or for a caution administered to an opponent.
Two points are scored:
for applying a correct hold and placing an opponent in danger for less than five seconds;
or if an opponent is in a momentary, accidental, or rolling fall.
Three points are scored for:
keeping an opponent in danger for five seconds;

or for a major technical hold that does not end by putting the opponent in immediate danger.

breaking a tie

A tie in points at the end of the bout is broken by considering in turn, until a difference is found:
first, the number of technical points awarded to each wrestler (i.e., ignoring points for cautions);
then, the number of holds awarded 4 points;
then the number awarded 3 points;
then the number awarded 2 points;
then who scored the first technical point.

elimination

The result of each bout is converted into a given number of penalty points, according to the table shown. When he reaches six penalty points, a contestant is eliminated (unless it is a win that takes his total over 6). Elimination rounds continue till only three wrestlers are left in the competition.

result of bout	penalty points
Win by a fall	0
Win by 12 or more points	0
Win by 8–11 points	$\frac{1}{2}$
Win by less than 8 points	1
Lose by a fall	4
Lose by 12 or more points	4
Lose by 8–11 points	$3\frac{1}{2}$
Lose by less than 8 points	3
Win by disqualification, injury, or forfeit	0
Lose by disqualification, injury or forfeit	4
Win by passivity (depends on number of cautions and technical points received by winner and loser)	0–2
Lose by passivity	4

the final

After the elimination rounds, only three contestants remain, as the finalists. If any of these finalists have not met in a previous round, they must now meet in a bout. But if they have met already, the penalty points recorded then are carried forward, and they do not meet again.

the result

The competition is won by the finalist with the fewest penalty points total from his bouts against the two other finalists. If two finalists have the same number of penalty points, then the one who won the bout they fought together is declared the winner. If three finalists have the same number, their performances throughout the competition are considered, until a difference is found, considering first penalty points, then number of victories, then number of victories by fall, then number by superiority, then least number of defeats, then least number of draw bouts, and finally least number of cautions received in the bouts of the final. Only if none of these procedures produces a result is a draw declared.

wrestling on edge of mat
When the wrestlers are
standing, if one foot of either
wrestler goes into the passivity
zone, the referee warns
"zone." The wrestlers must
then try to return toward the
middle of the mat, without
interrupting their wrestling
action. But the bout is
interrupted and restarted at
the mat center if they :
stop action while in the
passivity zone ;
stay there without action ;
or put, between them, more
than one foot in the zone
without action.
(They may begin action there
so long as only two feet,
between them, are in the zone.)
If one foot of either wrestler
goes out of the contest area
into the protection surface
area, the bout is also
interrupted and resumed at the
center of the mat. But the
points for any action still
stand, as long as it began in
a standing position in the
central wrestling area.
When the wrestlers are on the
ground, the bout is only
interrupted if the body of the
wrestler underneath goes into
the protection surface area.
(Even if both legs of both
wrestlers are into that area,
the bout can go on.) Also any
action that starts in the
passivity zone is good, and
if it carries into the protection
surface area the points still
stand.
If the body of the wrestler
underneath does go into the
protection surface area, the
restart is at the center of the
mat, with the contestants in

the "referee's position"
(below). The wrestler
underneath must kneel with
his hands and knees at least
20 centimeters apart, hands off
the mat. The uppermost
wrestler places his hands on
his opponent's shoulder
blades, with thumbs touching,
and the referee checks their
position before blowing his
whistle. Only then may the
wrestler underneath attack.
The uppermost wrestler may
not resume by jumping on his
opponent.

fouls
The rules of wrestling forbid :
stepping on an opponent's
feet (**a**) ;
touching his face between
eyebrows and mouth (**b**) ;
gripping his throat (**c**) ;
forcing an elbow or knee into
his stomach or abdomen (**d**) ;
pulling an opponent's hair,
flesh, ears, genitals, or costume ;
twisting his fingers or toes ;
brawling, kicking, throttling,
or pushing ;
applying holds liable to
endanger life, fracture limbs,
or torture an opponent into
submission ;
twisting an opponent's arm

more than 90 degrees;
applying head holds using both
hands;
applying head locks;
applying scissors grips by the
legs on an opponent's head,
neck, or body;
closing his arm and forearm
behind his back with pressure;
lifting an opponent from a
bridge to throw him onto the
mat (bridges must be pushed
down, and may not be
collapsed by pushing in the
direction of the head);
pinching or biting;
using an armbar applied to the
forearm, a three-quarter nelson

with both hands, or a chancery
hold;
gripping the mat;
or speaking to an opponent
during a bout.
The double nelson is permitted,
but must always be applied
from the side, and the legs
must not be used against the
opponent's body at the same
time.
In Greco–Roman wrestling it
is also forbidden to:
seize an opponent's legs (**e**);
or use the legs to push, lift,
or exert pressure through
contact on the opponent's
body (**f**).

passive obstruction
A wrestler commits passive
obstruction if, for example, he:
continually obstructs an
opponent's holds; continually
lies flat on his stomach on the
mat; wilfully runs off the mat;
or holds both an opponent's
hands.

cautions
Cautions are given for:
passive obstruction (after an
initial warning);
repeated retreats into the
passivity zone;
lack of discipline;
fouls and infringements of the
rules;
arguing with the judge or mat
chairman;
or making no action or points.
To caution a competitor, the
referee raises one arm and
holds the offender's wrist
with his other hand. After
two cautions, the mat
chairman co-opts another
official to assist him.
A contestant who has received
three cautions automatically
loses the bout. Cautions are
only valid, however, if they
are confirmed by a majority of
the three officials.

disqualification
A competitor may only be
disqualified from an entire
competition for a serious
offense, not for receiving
three or more cautions. The
vote of a co-opted fourth
official is needed for
disqualification.

On this page and the next are shown some of the more frequent and important incidents that can arise in competition wrestling. In each case the referee is using the sign language developed for international contests.

out (a)
This is a bad takedown because the head and shoulders of the wrestler underneath are off the edge of the mat. The bout will now be stopped and restarted. The referee is signaling "out."

restart (b)
A restart from the kneeling position in the center of the mat. The referee is about to allow the contestants to resume by blowing his whistle.

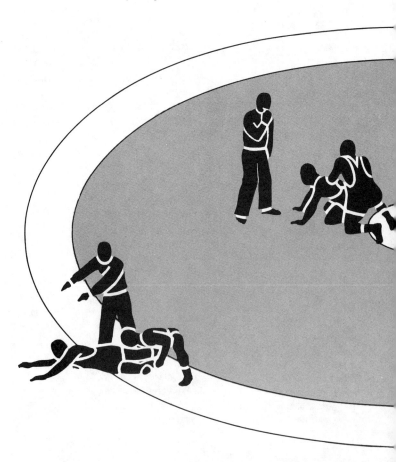

As well as using signals, referees in international matches may use recognized words in French to indicate different situations. Examples include:

attention (at-on-shi-on), meaning that a caution is about to be given.

avertissement (av-air-tees-mon), a caution;

contact (kon-tak), the order to a wrestler to place his hands on the opponent's back for the referee's position (see p. 54);

continue (kon-tee-new), the order to go on wrestling;

danger (don-shjay), indicating there is danger of a fall;

fin (fan), marking the end of the bout;

nul (nool), indicating a drawn bout;

passiveté (pas-iv-ee-tay), the warning for stalling (passive obstruction);

touche (toosh), meaning a fall;

victoire (vik-twahr), used to indicate the winner.

placing in danger (c)
The wrestler underneath has been placed in danger of a fall, since his back is toward the mat. The referee is indicating that the wrestler on top has scored two points.

fall (d)
Both the shoulders of the wrestler underneath are touching the mat. The referee is about to strike the mat to signal the fall.

Vigorous training is essential for wrestlers. The usual fitness exercises such as jumping rope and running help to develop stamina and physical agility. Practice drills establish reflex patterns of move and countermove. Weight training (see pp. 64–67) is very important in developing specific strength. But unique to wrestling are the bridging exercises. These help to develop a strong neck, which is one of the most vital of all physical attributes for a wrestler.

1

2

3

bridging with a partner (above)
Bridging-exercise training begins with work with a partner. One wrestler holds out his left forearm. The second grasps it (**1**) and drops back into a bridge (**2**), being supported by his partner. From this position, with practice, he will find that he can support himself. (**3**).

bridging alone (below)
This simple bridging exercise can be done without assistance. The wrestler puts his forehead on the floor with his legs apart and his hands behind his back (**1**).

After rocking to and fro on his head, he does a backward somersault into the bridge position (**2**), and there rocks backward and forward again, trying to touch the mat with his nose (**3**).

1

2

3

Breakdowns	Techniques used after a successful takedown to force an opponent onto his stomach or his side.
Catch-as-catch-can	Alternative name for freestyle wrestling.
Countering techniques	Methods used by a wrestler to overcome his opponent's holds.
Cumberland and Westmorland	Traditional style of wrestling practiced in the north of Britain. Contestants fight with their arms clasped behind each other's backs.
Freestyle	The most frequent and popular style of amateur wrestling today. Contestants may use all parts of their bodies, though certain potentially dangerous holds are forbidden.
Greco-Roman	A style of wrestling that developed in ancient Greece and Rome. Its rules are the same as those of freestyle, except that contestants may not use their legs or apply holds below the waist.

Hold	Any movement or technique applied by one wrestler on his opponent.
Pinning combinations	Techniques used after a successful breakdown, by which a wrestler tries to bring about a fall.
Placing in danger	A wrestler is said to be placed in danger of a fall when his opponent has almost forced him into the fall – if, for instance, his head and one of his shoulders are touching the floor. Points may be scored by the opponent according to how long the wrestler remains in danger.
Referee's position	The position taken up by the contestants on the mat after a bout has been interrupted: see p. 52
Sparring position	The position that wrestlers take up at the beginning of each bout or round.
Takedowns	Techniques used to force an opponent to the floor.

Young Dutch schoolboys
practice wrestling exercises
in a youth club in the 1930s.
The close contact of wrestling
and training brings its own
comradeship.

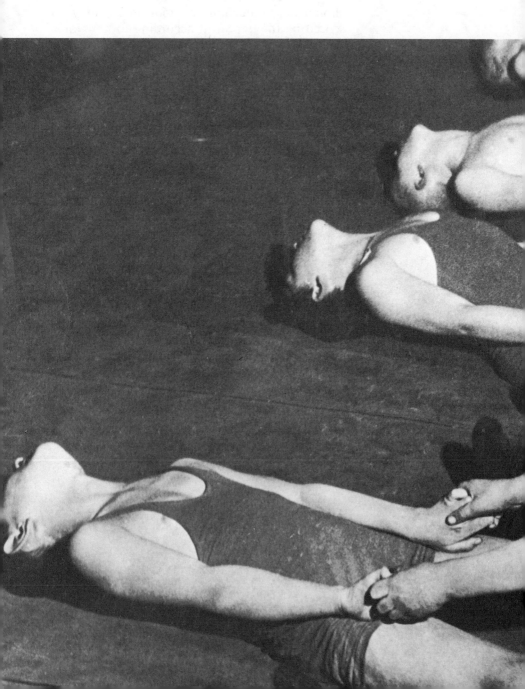

Weight-lifting is an excellent way of training for both boxing and wrestling. It helps to strengthen the muscles and increase all-round physical stamina and endurance. Remember, however, that weight-lifting is an organized sport with its own rules and regulations, and important safety precautions. Training with weights should be done under guidance and according to a properly worked out program: it is not just a matter of lifting the occasional barbell in a spare moment.

Never start lifting cold. Warm up first by running on the spot, touching your toes, and bending your knees.

Never stretch yourself beyond what you know you are capable of. If you are lifting a heavy barbell, ask spotters to stand at each end. Never get into a situation where you have to drop a heavy weight.

Always progress in the following way. For each exercise, choose a weight light enough for you to do a 5–5–5 repetition; that is, to do the exercise 15 times, in three groups of five, with enough pause between each group for you to get your breath back. Once you can do a 10–10–10 repetition with that weight, then you can increase it by 5%.

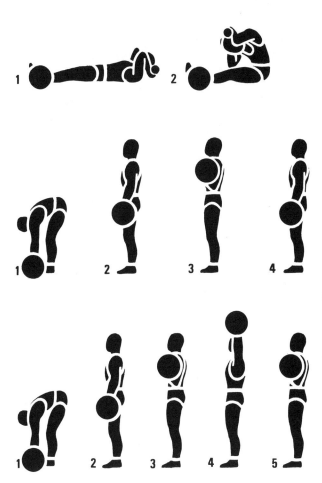

sit-up

Lie on your back on the floor and put your feet under a barbell. Place a light dumbell behind your neck (**1**), and hold it in place as you sit up (**2**), bending your head forward and down as far as possible. Return and repeat.

two-handed curl

Grasp the barbell with both hands, keeping the palms outward (**1**). Straighten, bringing the barbell to your thighs (**2**). Then lift it slowly to shoulder height without moving the upper arms (**3**). Lower it back to the thighs in the same way (**4**). For each repetition, repeat the last two movements.

dead lift and military press

Stand with your feet 12 to 18 inches apart. Grasp the barbell with both hands, shoulder width apart (**1**), straighten up (**2**), and lift it to your chest (**3**). Then, with arms outstretched, push it to arm's length above your head (**4**), before lowering it back to your chest (**5**). For each repetition, repeat the last two movements.

bench press

Lie on your back on a bench holding a barbell close to your chest (**1**). Stretch your arms out fully (**2**), and then return them to their original position. Repeat. A spotter should stand by your head as you do this exercise.

In competition weight-lifting, contestants have to lift the barbell in two different ways: the snatch, and the jerk (or "clean and jerk").

snatch
Grasp the bar with both hands, palms down, and lift it in a single movement straight above your head, with both arms fully stretched up, at the same time bending the knees into a crouching position. The bar must pass along the body in a continuous movement. Unlimited time is then allowed for "recovery" – that is, to move from the crouching position to one in which the body is fully erect. After recovery, remain motionless, with arms and legs extended and feet on the same line.
The lifter may not:
pause during the lift;
turn his wrists over until the bar has passed over the top of his head;
extend the arms unevenly or incompletely;
or finish with a press-out.

clean and jerk
Grasp the bar with both hands, palms down, and lift it in a single movement to the shoulders, crouching at the same time. Then rest the bar on the collar bones, chest, or fully bent arms. This completes the clean. Unlimited time is then allowed for the "recovery" – that is, to return the feet to the same line and straighten the legs. At this time the lifter may also:
lower the bar onto his shoulders;
withdraw his thumbs or unhook from the bar;
and change the width of his grip.
To execute the jerk bend: and then straighten your legs and then fully stretch; your arms straight above your head. Another "recovery" of the feet position is then permitted before you stand motionless. Any apparent effort from the shoulders, including lowering the body or further bending of the knees, constitutes a "no lift."

Open grip   Simple grip   Hook grip

The martial arts of the orient can be divided into two distinct types: hard and soft. Those in the hard category employ techniques that are essentially forceful: a competitor uses his own strength and body weight to strike an opponent or to block his moves. Sudden movements and blows are all-important. Sports in the soft category are a complete contrast. In these, avoiding action is the key, and contestants try to harness their opponent's force to their own advantage, often by throwing him to the ground.

All the oriental martial arts were first developed as methods of self-defense. Today they are practiced almost exlusively as competitive sports. In this book, the techniques, equipment, and dress described all apply to the sports alone. They are not appropriate for self-defense.

Judo is a sport in the "soft" category. Force is never met with force; instead, a competitor gives way to his opponent's initial attack, and uses his resulting loss of control to throw him off balance. Another of the better-known soft sports is aikido. In this, too, force is met with avoiding action, not by counter force.

The different oriental combat sports all have certain things in common. They all develop great bodily control – in balance, agility, strength, speed, and precision of movement. As a counterpart to this, they all see themselves as ways to mental self-control. This self-discipline is backed up by outside discipline: the training is traditionally surrounded by ritual, and the teacher is a figure of great authority. The student also has to accept that the necessary physical control takes a long time to learn. So although these are combat sports, free-fighting may not be allowed until the student is well advanced. Instead, training itself is highly disciplined – consisting of set movements that must be practiced until perfect. As the student progresses, these movements are strung together in long chains called kata. Learning the movements admits him to a higher grade, marked by a different colored belt. So he progresses from the white belt of the novice to the black belt of the adept. All this helps distinguish these sports from mere self-defense techniques – which, in contrast, are ideally as simple as possible, and usable by anyone.

Most important among the hard oriental martial arts is karate. This is an offensive sport, in which contestants attack by striking and kicking one another. No actual harm is done, however, for all movements are controlled so that they stop just short of hurting the opponent.

Judo

Judo means "the gentle way." This may seem a strange description for something that set out to be the most efficient system of self-defense, and is still a highly competitive sport. But if you substitute "easier" for "gentle," the phrase becomes clearer. The founder of judo, a Japanese professor called Jigoro Kano, had studied the ancient Japanese jujitsu styles of fighting, and from these, in 1880, formulated a new style of his own – with a philosophy to go with it. It was, in fact, later taken up as a training style by the Japanese army, and even used by soldiers in combat. But the real success of judo came in another way, through its acceptance in Japan as a system of fighting that could be taught as a sport in schools. So it was as a sport that judo was to gain international recognition – in the West especially after the Second World War.

Jigoro Kano believed that every problem should be dealt with by "the highest or most efficient use of mental as well as physical energy," to quote his own words. He also believed that the techniques developed by judo would improve an individual in every aspect of his life, and help him to live more rationally. Today, judo devotees are not necessarily concerned with their art as part of a philosophical system. Yet who can deny that the mental and physical agility and control that it requires may not help an individual to a more balanced life?

Throughout this chapter on the oriental unarmed combat sports, the names of any techniques mentioned appear in English. But the commands and other terms that occur in competition have been left in Japanese, which is the language used. An English translation of each of these is given, though, both in the text and in the glossary on pp. 114–115.

The next few pages set out the basics of judo. They do not teach you how to do judo – that would be impossible in such a small space, and dangerous too. It should only be learned by joining a class under a qualified teacher. Never try to teach yourself – you or someone else may well get hurt.

In judo you use the force of your opponent's own efforts to draw him off balance. Then you can throw him to the ground. So balance – and how to fall when *you* are thrown – are usually the first things you have to learn as a judo pupil – and perhaps the most difficult to master.

a   b   c   d

stance
a If you stand in an ordinary way, your control over your balance is not very good. You can resist a push or pull from the side – but not one from the front or back.
b Just by changing the position of your feet, your control greatly improves. This is the basic practice or T stance – so called because the rear foot is directly behind the front foot and at right angles to it. Now you can resist a push or pull from any direction.
c The other ways of making your stance stronger are crouching, to give a lower center of gravity, and spreading your feet to give a wider base.
d Here all the elements of a strong stance are combined: feet at right angles and widely spread, and body low.

simple back fall

Falling practice is vital, but must progress in very easy stages. For a simple back fall, crouch, and let yourself roll gently back. Strike the mat hard with your arms just before your back hits the mat. Note how this breaks the momentum. Your head should not hit the mat.

simple side fall

Crouch on one leg, pivoting to that side, and roll back on your buttocks. Strike the mat hard with your nearest arm just before your back hits the mat.

simple forward fall

Drop gently to your knees, then fall forward. Strike the mat with your hands and forearms. Keep your hands directly in front of your face, and your elbows turned slightly out. Only toes, knees, and forearms should touch the mat.

basic side roll

With feet shoulder-width apart, put your right hand straight in front of you on the mat, and the left a little behind it. Get your weight onto your left foot and right hand. Raise your right foot, and roll down your left arm, onto shoulder, back, and right side, slapping the mat with right arm and leg at the end.

fighting position

In judo, you grapple with your opponent by taking hold of his costume. Your right hand grips the left lapel of his jacket; your left hand grips the underside of the right arm of his jacket. The drawings show:
a the usual position for practice throws in training;
b the usual contest position.

weakening your opponent's stance

You may need to set off your opponent's loss of balance by breaking the strength of his stance. Techniques include twisting him to one side (**a**), pulling or pushing him into a tilt (**b**), lifting him (**c**), or a combination of these.

throwing

You can throw your opponent over your foot, leg, hip, or shoulder. The drawings show tsurikomi-ashi (foot sweep), one of the basic throws. The opponent is drawn forward (**1**) until he is off balance. Then, as you pivot (**2**), he is tripped by your left foot, and thrown over your leg (**3**). Note how he raises his arm (**4**), ready to break his fall.

1

countering

These drawings of utsuri-goshi (changing hip throw) show how you can use your opponent's efforts against him. Your opponent plans to throw you over his hip. As he comes in (**1**), you drop your right hand to his belt. When he tries to lift for the throw, you use this effort to lift him high into the air (**2**). Then you quickly move in front of him (**3**), so that he falls onto your hip (**4**). From there you can easily throw him to the floor (**5**).

1

ground techniques

These drawings show examples of the holds and armlocks used when an opponent has been brought to the floor. They require skill and a great deal of practice, and should not be attempted without supervision.

release signal

If your opponent – or your partner if you are practicing – taps on either the floor or your own body, you must release him immediately. This is a universally recognized safety signal.

2

3

4

2

3

4

5

Balance, coordination and dexterity are all qualities that must be developed by the judo enthusiast. Endless practice of the falls and throws is the main way forward. But regular footwork and falling exercises, such as those shown here, are useful too.

gliding (above)
This helps to develop balance in the T stance position (see p. 74). From the opening stance (**1**), step out with right foot (**2**). Then put your weight on right foot, and slide left foot forward (**3**). Finally step back on left foot (**4**), and return to (**1**). Maintain the T stance throughout. The partner is shown as a reference point.

hopping (below)
For rapid movement, practice this hopping sequence – very useful if you need to switch feet quickly for a throw. Mark an X on the floor: whichever foot is taking the weight of your body should stay on the X. Start with hands on hips, weight on left foot, and right foot extended (**1**). Hop onto right foot and extend left (**2**). Return to starting position (**3**).

Hop onto right foot and extend left foot back (**4**). Hop onto left foot and extend right foot back (**5**). Hop onto right foot and extend left foot forward (**6**). Hop onto left foot and extend right foot forward (**7**). Hop onto right foot and extend left foot to side (**8**). Return to starting position (**9**). On each hop, the ball of the extended foot can give slight support.

neck-body twist

This is a good but difficult exercise for the neck. Start with hands behind back, head on mat, and legs spread out (**1**). Then cross one leg over the other (**2**), pivot on top of head, and roll over so the back is bridged above the floor (**3**). Finish by crossing one leg over the other and rolling back to (**1**). Throughout, hands and hips should not touch the floor.

backward and forward roll

Start in seated position (**1**). Roll back, twisting head to one side and placing hands on mat palm up (**2**). Roll over (**3**), and finish in kneeling position (**4**). To return, get up and bend over with palms down on floor (**5**). Roll forward (**6**), and finish in the starting position (**7**).

The International Judo Federation was founded in 1954, and since then judo has made rapid progress as a combat sport with standardized rules and international recognition. World championships have been held since 1956, and in 1964 judo became an Olympic sport for the first time.

the mat
In international competitions the contest area (shiaijo) is 9 to 10 meters square. It is bordered by a red danger area 1 meter wide, and this in turn is surrounded by a safety area of green matting to prevent injuries. The entire competition area measures 14 to 16 meters square. The contest must be fought within the limits of the contest area.

officials
In charge of the contest are:
a the referee, who generally stays within the contest area and conducts the bout; and
b two judges, who sit at opposite corners of the safety area and assist the referee.

b

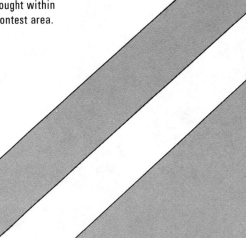

a

weight limits	**men**	**women**
Judo competitions are divided	60kg	48kg
into weight categories, just as	65	52
boxing and wrestling are. The	71	56
category weight limits	78	61
are given alongside.	86	66
	95	72
	over 95	over 72

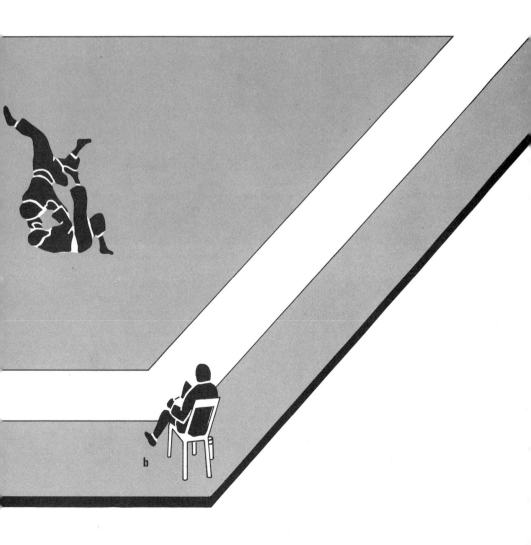

b

dress

Contestants must wear a white or off-white costume (judogi). The jacket must cover the hips, and is usually slit for about 18 centimeters up each side. It has continuous strengthened lapels about 4 centimeters wide, and below the waistline and at the armpits there must be reinforced stitching. Sleeves must be loose, and cover more than half the forearm.

The pants must be loose, and should cover over half the lower leg. The belt is used to fasten the jacket at the waist, and must be long enough to go twice round the body. It is tied with a large square knot, and its ends should be about 15 centimeters long. In competition, contestants wear either a white or a red sash, to distinguish them.

start

At the start the contestants stand about 4 meters apart, facing each other, and make a standing bow. The contest is then started immediately by the referee, who shouts ''hajime'' (''begin''). Contestants must begin all movements in a standing position within the contest area.

duration

The length of the contest is arranged in advance, and must be between three and 20 minutes. The contest may be temporarily halted on a call from the referee: if the contestants are about to leave the contest area; if either has been injured, or an accident has happened; after a foul; or if one is imminent; to disentangle unproductive holds; or to allow a costume to be adjusted.

At the end of the contest, the competitors return to their starting places, and make a standing bow to each other after the decision has been announced.

scoring

The competitors are judged on their throwing techniques (nagewaza) and holding techniques (katamewaza). Violations of the rules are also taken into account.

A contestant who gains an ippon (one point) wins outright. An ippon is awarded for:

a a throw of considerable force;

a

b lifting the opponent from the mat to shoulder height;

c making an effective stranglehold or lock; or

d maintaining a hold for 30 seconds.

If a competitor just fails to make an ippon, he may be awarded a waza-ari. Two waza-ari are equivalent to one ippon. If a contestant wins only one waza-ari but his opponent also commits a serious violation against him, he wins outright too.

b

If neither contestant gains an ippon, a win by superiority (yuseigachi) is declared if a contestant was awarded a waza-ari or displayed a technique close to one.

If no decision can be reached on the basis of the competitors' performance, their attitude in the contest and their skill in technique are taken into account.

c

The judges may award a draw, and a bout may be lost by default. In the event of injury, illness, or accident, the judges and referee decide the result.

d

a

b

c

d

fouls

A competitor may not:

a sweep an attacking opponent's supporting leg from the inside (though he may hook his instep);

b try to throw an opponent by entwining one leg around one of his opponent's legs (kawazugake);

c deliberately fall back when an opponent is clinging to his back and when either contestant is controlling the other's movements;

d adopt an excessively defensive attitude, either physically or simply by not attacking;

e pull his opponent down in order to start groundwork;

f take hold of his opponent's leg or foot in order to change to ne-waza (ground techniques), unless exceptional skill is shown;

g break his opponent's fingers back;

h continuously hold his opponent's costume on the same side with both hands, or hold the belt at the bottom of his jacket;

put a hand, arm, foot, or leg directly on his opponent's face, or take his judogi in his mouth;

while lying on his back, maintain a leg hold around his opponent's neck, if the latter manages to stand or get to his knees so he could lift the holder up;

apply lock joints (kansetsu-waza), except at the elbow joint;

apply leg scissors to trunk, neck or head;

kick his opponent's hand
to make him let go;
endanger his opponent's
neck or spine;

lift an opponent who is lying
on his back off the mat so as
to drive him onto it again;
intentionally go outside the
contest area, or force his
opponent to go outside it;
seize the inside of his
opponent's sleeve or the
bottom of his pants;
stand continuously with his
fingers interlocked with his
opponent's;
deliberately disarrange his
own costume;
wind his belt or jacket
around his opponent;
disregard the referee;
make derogatory remarks or
gestures;
or do anything contrary to the
spirit of judo.

penalties
The referee may award four
types of penalty. In order of
increasing gravity, these are:
shido, chui, keikoku, and
hansoko-make
(disqualification). Before
awarding the last two, the
referee must consult the
judges and obtain a majority
decision.
Each of the first three
penalties is taken into
account in the judges'
assessment at the end of the
contest. Hansoko-make applies
if a competitor commits a
major foul or repeatedly
ignores the referee's
warnings about fouling.

e

f

g

h

Karate

Karate is one of Japan's most successful exports. But in origin it is not Japanese at all. The ancient unarmed combat styles of that country show up in modern judo and aikido. Karate, instead, derives from traditional Chinese techniques now 1,500 years old. From China, these spread to Korea and the island of Okinawa. But only in this century did a teacher from Okinawa go to Japan, and establish the beginnings of modern karate.

Something has been said already about "hard" and "soft" combat styles. As a sport, karate is in general the hardest – the most forceful – of those in this chapter. But there are many styles of karate, all slightly different. While some emphasize strength above all else, others give more scope for speed and agility. In fact, the newcomer to karate will find a bewildering variety of names. In general, though, the styles first set down in Japan by Okinawan and Korean teachers tend to be hard: examples include *shotokan*, *goju ryu*, *uechi-ryu*, and *kyokushinkai*. Derivations – such as *wadoryu* and *shukokai* – founded by the Japanese themselves, tend to be softer, and more suited to competition conditions.

Something also needs to be said about kung fu. This is the name often given by westerners to Chinese fighting styles. (It is not a name that the Chinese use.) Some of these are very like modern karate, for they are descended from the same tradition, although not so often used in competition as a sport. But the range of Chinese styles also includes very soft traditions, such as *t'ai chi ch'uan* – never practiced as a combat sport, but widely used as a recipe for health and well-being, while highly effective as self-defense in the hands of a master.

On this page and the next the differences between the two forms of karate are made clear. Sport karate is a contest in which the participants do not have to strike, let alone hurt, each other. Yet for this reason, it is far more testing, and demands far more agility and control, than mere self-defense.

 Partners in sport karate respect each other, and display this respect by bowing to each other at the start of each match.

 Punches and kicks in sport karate do not have to land, to score – and if they land with more than a light touch, they count as fouls.

 The only weapons used in sport karate are the hands and feet.

In sport karate, only kicks aimed at the top and middle parts of an opponent's body win points. In self-defense, low kicks are more common.

In sport karate, dangerous techniques, such as blows to the eyes, are illegal. In self-defense, any means that will be effective may have to be used.

Contestants in sport karate must abide by strict rules of play.

Throttling, body crashing, and squeezing are all forbidden in sport karate.

The next few pages introduce some basic karate techniques. Karate aims to develop all the body's potential for controlled force. The head, elbows, and knees may all be used as weapons; but most techniques – especially those seen in competition – involve blows with the hand or foot.

Always remember that control is as much a part of karate as force. In contest, blows must strike so that full power is focused to within two inches of your opponent – yet he must be touched only lightly or (better) not at all.

practice
There are two main kinds of karate practice: group, and partner. The first involves doing techniques as one of a group, all moving together. The second involves trying them out with a mock opponent. In each case, both single techniques and set sequences can be practiced.

basic stances
For the forward stance (**a**), your feet should be about twice shoulder width apart. The hips are turned forward, the rear foot slightly out. The rear heel is flat on the ground, the rear leg tense and unbent. This position is good for attack.
For the backward stance (**b**), your body is half turned away from your opponent. The rear foot points out sideways, both legs are bent, and weight is on the rear foot. This position is good for defense.
The horse stance (**c**) is good for attacks to the side, the cat stance (**d**) for fast movement. The ready stance (**e**) is used before going into a fighting stance.

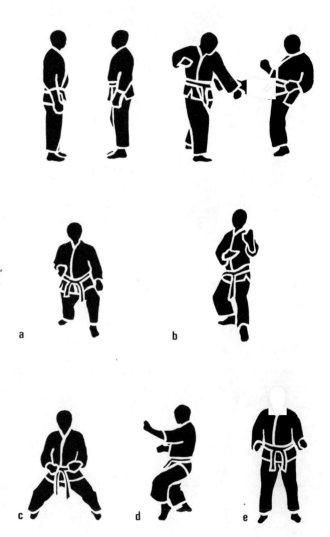

the fist

Karate hand blows may use the side, palm, or fingers, but the fist is the main weapon. The karate fist is very tightly clenched, with the thumb well locked over (**a**). Contact is with the knuckles of the first and middle fingers (**b**).

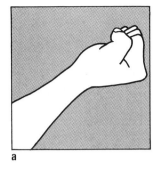
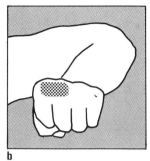

a   b

basic straight delivery

This starts from your waist (**1**), with the fist upside down. Punch in a straight line to the target, your elbow brushing close past your body (**2**). The fist automatically turns right way up just before impact. On impact (**3**), fist, wrist, and arm are all in line. The return is as fast as the punch – an immediate rebound.

1   2   3

reverse punch

From the basic stance (**1**), drive your rear fist forward to the target, turning your body into the punch so that on impact (**2**) the hips are turned to face the opponent. Keep your shoulders back. As you punch, bring your other hand back to a clenched position at your waist.

1   2

lunge punch

This can be delivered from further away. From the basic stance (**1**), you slide your rear foot forward, keeping your hips low; then punch (**2**) just as the right foot settles on the ground. Be careful to keep your body upright.

1   2

kicks

Kicks are more powerful than punches, but slower and harder to control, and they can leave the kicker unbalanced and defenseless. In karate the main parts of the foot used for kicking are the ball of the foot (**a**), instep (**b**), side (**c**), and heel (**d**).

front kick

From the forward stance (**1**), bring your rear leg high toward your chest (**2**), and snap it straight out in front (**3**), tilting your hips down into the movement. The strike is with the ball of the foot: keep the toes curled back. Let the leg rebound at once on its own momentum, bringing it right back to (**1**) without losing balance.

side thrust kick

From the backward stance (**1**), go back onto your rear leg, bringing your front foot up to your rear knee (**2**). Then stamp your leg out, to strike with the ball of the foot (**3**), swiveling on your rear foot so you turn sideways into the kick. Bring the leg back under control to (**2**) and then (**1**).

roundhouse kick

From the forward stance, bring your rear knee up, foot turned out, so the lower leg is almost parallel with the ground (**1a** and **b**). Then swing the foot in an arc to the target, while pivoting on your other foot (**2**). Strike with ball of foot or instep. Return under control to (**1**), then to ground.

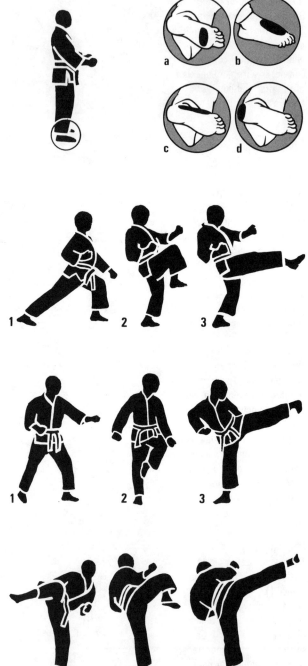

upward block

Blocking techniques are vital for successful defense. Upward blocks meet attacks to the chest and face. The blocking arm swings up from the waist (**1**) across the chest (**2**), then twists hard above your head (**3**) so the palm of the hand faces out. The other hand comes across chest (**2**). and back to a fist at the waist.

downward block

This meets attacks to the abdomen. The blocking arm comes up to your opposite ear (**1**), then hard down across the body (**2**). Meanwhile the other hand comes across the abdomen (**1**), then back to a fist at the waist (**2**).

inner block

This blocks attacks to the chest. The blocking arm comes across to your opposite armpit (**1**), then rotates back hard across the body, turning from the elbow (**2**). The blow is deflected with the thumb side of the forearm.

countering

Blocking can lead into a strong counterattack. The illustrations show an upward block to a punch (**1**), followed by a reverse punch attack to the chest (**2**).

Apart from teaching techniques and sequences, karate training aims to develop strength, speed, precision, and physical flexibility. Constant practice of the various kicks and blows is the main method used, but the exercises described here are also important.

flexibility

Sessions often begin with hand-shaking (**a**) and head-circling (**b**). Then in body-bending (**c**) you try to touch each knee with your head. Leg stretching (**d**) begins from a standing spread-leg position: you try to bend one knee as far as possible without bending the other one or lifting the foot from the ground. Stretching exercises with a partner (**e**) are also used.

strength

A punch bag (**a**) is often used. If there is no way of hanging or supporting it, it can be held by a partner. But the traditional equipment is a makiwara, or **striking board** (**b** and **c**), its front covered with straw or spongy material. Punching this hardens the hands at the same time.

speed and precision

Speed and aim are improved by kicking and punching at a ball suspended at the right height on a line (**a**). Control is developed by punching and kicking at a partner's hand (**b**). Use full power but focus the blow so that it stops just as it touches the target.

c

d

e

b

c

balance

Standing on one leg is an important balancing exercise. From the starting position (**a**), you should move your leg and body into several different positions, holding each one briefly (**b**), before you bring your leg back under control to the floor.

a

b

Competitive sport karate rose to international significance in the 1960s, and in 1970 the World Union of Karate Organizations was formed. Besides setting down the basic rules for all karate competitions, WUKO has introduced regular world championships, and hopes for Olympic status for the sport in the 1980s.

match area
Contests take place on a flat surface 8 meters square, which must be completely free from obstacles.

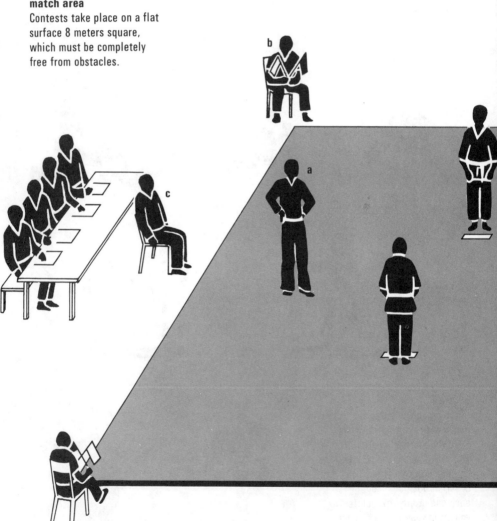

officials

These include:
a the referee, who observes the fight from inside the match area;
b four judges, one seated at each corner of the area; and
c the arbitrator, who sits to one side of the area.
In addition, there are one or more timekeepers, recordkeepers, and administrators.

referee

The referee conducts the match, awards points, announces fouls, issues warnings, and takes disciplinary measures. In the event of a draw, he casts the deciding vote. He may also extend the match when necessary.

The referee receives advice from the judges. If only one judge signals him, the referee may ignore him, but if two or more do so he must suspend the match and consult them.

judges

Each judge has two flags, one red and one white, and a whistle. He uses these to signal, for example:
a point scored;
a foul or imminent foul;
or a contestant outside the contest area.
The judges also indicate if they disagree with the referee, and if they are in a majority they may overrule him.
The judges continuously evaluate the performance of the contestants throughout the match, and use this evaluation in giving their votes if victory has to be awarded by majority decision.

arbitrator

The arbitrator judges, protests, directs the timekeeper and recordkeeper, and oversees the contest.

dress

Contestants must wear a lightweight white suit (karate-gi), with a colored belt (obi) indicating their formal grade. For identification during the contest, one competitor fastens a white string to his belt, the other a red. Metallic objects such as badges may not be worn, and protective or safety devices only with permission.

scoring

A contestant scores by using a recognized competition karate technique, well delivered, to the permitted scoring area of his opponent's body (shown below).
But actual physical contact is not necessary to score. Points are awarded for controlled techniques that finish within 2 inches of the target surface. In fact, contestants may only touch each other lightly on the body, and only very lightly on the face and head. Excessive physical contact always results in disqualification.

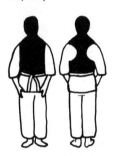

winning

You can win:
by scoring one ippon (a full point) or two waza-ari (half points) before your opponent does;
by your opponent being disqualified;
or (if neither of these occurs) on the decision of the judges and referee.
(In some matches you need two full points to win: see p. 101.)

ippon

An ippon (one point) is awarded for a blow that is struck with good style, good attitude, vigor, zanshin (constant alertness of mind), proper timing, and correct distancing. Tsuki (thrusts), uchi (snaps), ate (hits), and keri (kicks), are all permitted

waza-ari

Waza-ari (half a point) is awarded for a blow that is less correct but still effective – if, for example, the opponent is moving away from the blow, or the blow is slightly off target, or is delivered from a slightly unstable position.

other ippons

An ippon may be awarded for a less powerful blow if:
the attack was delivered just as the opponent began to move toward the attacker;
the attack was delivered just as the opponent was thrown off balance by the attacker;
a combination of effective blows was applied;
a combination of tsuki and keri or of tsuki and nage (throw) techniques was used;
the opponent lost his fighting spirit and turned his back on the attacker;
the attack was delivered to a defenseless part of the target.

not ippons

An ippon is not awarded if an attacker does not deliver the blow the moment he has seized or thrown his opponent. If both contestants hit target simultaneously, neither point is scored.
Scoring techniques delivered simultaneously with the end of time signal are counted, as are techniques delivered when the attacker is within the match area but his opponent is outside it.

victory by decision

If neither contestant gains an ippon, the judges may declare victory by hanteigachi (superiority) if a competitor has scored half a point, or on the basis of the following factors:
the number of retreats outside the match area;
any warnings due to fouls;
the comparative vigor and fighting spirit shown by the contestants;
their comparative skill and ability;
the number of attacking moves each has made;
and the comparative excellence of the strategy used.

procedure

At the start of the match, the referee takes up position in the match area. The contestants stand facing each other with their toes touching the starting line and bow to one another. When the referee calls "shobu ippon hajime" the match begins.

duration

Matches normally last two minutes but may be extended to three or five to achieve a result. Time taken during injury or inquiry stoppages does not count toward the match time.

The timekeeper signals with a gong or buzzer 30 seconds before the end of the match ("atoshi boraku"), and again at the end.

halting the match

If an ippon is scored, the referee signals "yame," and the contestants return to their starting lines. The referee returns to his position, raises his left or right hand to indicate the victor, and calls out the name of the technique used to score. The contestants then bow to each other, and the match ends.

If a waza-ari is scored, the referee calls "yame" and the contestants return to the starting lines. The referee returns to his position, and, pointing to the scorer, calls out "waza-ari" and the scoring technique used. Then – unless one contestant now has two waza-ari the referee calls out, "tsuzukete hajime" and the match starts again.

temporary halts

The referee may call "yame" and halt the match if: infighting not based on effective techniques develops; one or both contestants are out of the match area; he wishes a contestant to adjust his dress; he sees that a contestant is about to commit a foul; a competitor is injured or becomes ill; a rule is broken; or a judge signals.

If necessary, the referee may consult the judges and return the contestants to their starting lines before allowing the match to continue.

If a halt lasts for more than 10 seconds it is not counted in the match time.

no score

If a match ends and neither competitor has scored an ippon, the referee calls out "yame," and he and the contestants then return to their positions. After the judges have had sufficient time to make a decision, the referee calls "hantei" and blows his whistle. The judges then indicate their votes by signaling with their flags. The referee has a casting vote if necessary.

injuries

Injury can be self inflicted by accident, or due to a foul by an opponent. In the latter case the opponent is disqualified, and the injured competitor wins the match even though he may be unable to continue. But a contestant loses if he refuses to continue, or requests permission to quit, after an injury insufficiently serious to disable him. He also loses if he cannot continue, or asks permission to quit, for reasons other than injury.

If neither contestant is responsible for an injury, or if both are injured at the same time and both are responsible, then if one contestant quits he is declared the loser.

If an injury is unintentional – if, for example, a contestant runs onto a controlled blow – the decision rests with the judges.

If both withdraw through injuries not attributable to either contestant, the match is declared a draw.

internationals

Some matches are fought for the best of three points: internationals are always on this basis. The referee begins the match with "shobu sanbon hajime." The first contestant to reach two full points wins. Individual contestants are paired off for fights, and the team with the greatest number of individual winners wins the whole match. Ties are won by the team with the greater number of ippons, then (if there is still a tie) the greater number of waza-ari and wins by decision. Fouls and disqualifications count as ippons. If there is still a tie, an extra match is held.

extra match

This takes place between a chosen representative from each team, lasts for two minutes, and is repeated until a winner emerges. After two repeats, each contestant is replaced by another team member. If after a number of extra matches the result is still inconclusive, the panel of judges may decide the result of the match by conference.

protests

A contestant's team officer may protest against a decision by appealing to the arbitrator, who then consults the referee and judges.

fouls

The following are fouls:

a full contact attacks on the body other than the arms and legs;

b dangerous techniques, such as blows to the eyes or testicles;

c dangerous throws;

d persistent attacks directly on the shin;

e full contact attacks on the hips, knee joints, or insteps;

f unnecessary grabbing, clinching, or body crashing;

excessive moving out of the match area, or moves that waste time;

ignoring the rules of the contest;

and unsportsmanlike behavior.

penalties

A foul may result in:

a private warning by the referee in a quiet voice (chui);

a public warning by the referee in a loud voice (hansoku-chui);

or disqualification (hansoku) also announced by the referee.

disqualification

If a competitor continues to foul after being warned by the referee he is disqualified. Disqualification may also be imposed if a contestant:

fails to obey the referee;

becomes so overexcited that he can be considered a danger to his opponent;

breaks the rules with malicious intent;

or breaks the match rules in some other serious way.

Black-belts cooperate in an
outdoor demonstration of
karate techniques

Aikido

For over 800 years members of the Minamoto family of Japan passed down in secret, from generation to generation, a system of self-defense that had been developed by a great samurai general in the 12th century. In the early 1900s this knowledge was inherited by Professor Morihei Uyeshiba, and from it he developed aikido: "the way of harmony of spirit." Later one of his pupils, Kenji Tomiki, added some further modification of his own. The end result was a fast, mobile form of combat: as in judo, force is not met with counter force, but with avoiding action. The techniques used are very different from those of judo, however. Instead of grappling closely with an opponent to throw him across one's body, the aikidoist tends to work at arm's length – throwing an attacker through arm holds that act on the wrist and elbow joints. In fact, of all the combat sports in this book, it is aikido that places the greatest emphasis on victory through non-aggression.

A high-ranking aikido adept demonstrates a spectacular throwing technique.

Rules of aikido

One of the ways in which the Tomiki school of aikido differs from the original Uyeshiba school is in including an element of competition. Today the aikidoist can compete not only in the *kata* – a purely formal sequence of set moves – but also in three types of free-fighting event: *ninin dori, tanto randori,* and *randori kyoghi.* Aikido is not yet so well established, internationally, as other forms of combat sport; but its popularity is growing very rapidly.

match area

This should be at least 9 meters square, surrounded by a safety area.

dress

Dress is the same as for judo. For identification, one contestant wears a red belt (or a red string or tape attached to his belt), the other a white. Metal badges, jewelry, etc., are prohibited.

officials

For kata and ninin dori, one senior judge and two or more assistant judges are needed. For tanto randori and randori kyoghi, there is a referee within the competition area, and two judges at opposite corners. A scorer and a timekeeper are required at all competitions.

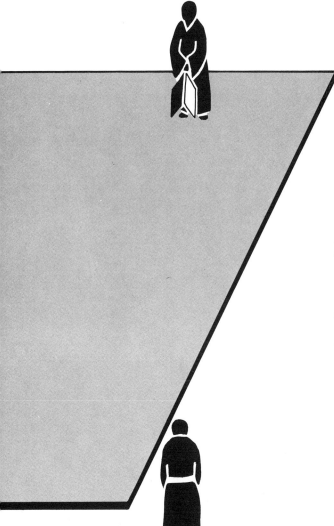

terms used

Terms used in Aikido include:
hajime, begin;
soremade, finish (of round or match);
yame or matte, stop (the contestants must return to their starting positions and timing is interrupted);
ippon, one point;
tanto ippon, one point for a knife strike;
waza-ari, half a point;
waza-ari awasette ippon, a half point that brings a competitor's total up to one full point;
hantei, a call for the score or for judgment;
hikkiwake, a draw;
chui, warning for fouling.

Kata

In *kata*, the two participants work together in a set, non-competitive routine of defense and attack. They are judged on the correctness and style with which the *kata* is performed. This is not combat, of course. But *kata* routines do set out, in a formal way, the basic combat techniques. Those illustrated on this page are all from the *randori no kata*, which sums up the basic moves for free-fighting in the Tomiki aikido style.

general procedure
One participant acts as tori (thrower), the other as uke (attacker). They stand 4 meters apart, facing joseki (the chief guest), and bow. Then they turn to face each other, and begin when "hajime" is called out. At the end, the senior judge calls "hantei" and the judges display their scores for the joint performance. These are added up by the recorder. The participants then turn to joseki, bow, and leave the area.

assessment
Performances should be polished, well paced, smooth, continuous, purposeful, and coordinated. The participants must show a good understanding of their kata and of each other.

scoring
Each judge can give up to 10 points. Scores may be given to one decimal place.

winning
The winning pair are those receiving the highest joint score for their kata.

randori no kata
This important *kata* is divided into four sections:
a) five attack techniques;
b) five elbow techniques;
c) four wrist-twisting techniques; and
d) three "floating techniques"

Alongside, one example of each is illustrated and briefly described, to give a general idea of aikido techniques. But never attempt any of these without expert supervision. In the first place, you are unlikely to be successful: the handholds involved have deliberately not been illustrated in detail, and can only be learned from a qualified aikido instructor. More important, aikido techniques, if misapplied, can easily break wrists and elbows, or send a partner crashing uncontrollably to the floor.

attacking technique
From the basic aikido stance
(**1**), you step outside the
attacking arm, and deflect it
with both hands – one at the
wrist and one at the elbow –
spinning the attacker round
(**2**). Moving quickly to his
side, you put your hands on
his shoulders, then step back
to your left, pulling the
attacker to the ground (**3**).

elbow technique
As the attacker reaches for
your chin, you catch his wrist
between your hands, using the
little finger edges (**1**).
Keeping your arms straight,
you step in and turn, bringing
the attacker's arm round (**2**).
Then you lock the twisted arm
to your chest, as you step
away (**3**).

wrist-twisting technique
You have grasped your
attacker's hand and wrist, but
he has managed to keep his
elbow turned down (**1**). So
you quickly change your grip,
moving to his other side (**2**).
You circle your arms in a
counterclockwise direction,
and your attacker goes over
(**3**).

floating technique
You move in and check the
attacker's right arm (**1**). Then
you step back and bring his
arm down in front of you, with
a slight twist (**2**), bringing
your attacker to the floor (**3**).

Tanto randori

For *tanto randori*, the attacker is armed with a dummy rubber knife, while his opponent, the defender, is unarmed. There are two rounds, each lasting a minute, and at the end of the first the competitors reverse roles. The use of "knife" techniques in *tanto randori* has made it a little controversial, but the whole emphasis of aikido training here is on defense against the knife attack.

procedure
The two contestants and the referee stand at the edge of the competition area, facing joseki, and bow. The two contestants then face each other at the center of the area, 4 meters apart. The contestant who is to attack in the first round stands to the right of the referee. Before each round, the attacker collects the knife from the referee.

On the command "rei" the contestants bow to one another. Each round begins on the command "hajime," ends on "yame," and may be interrupted by the command "matte" or "yame."

After the second round, the referee calls "hantei," and the recorder announces each contestant's score. The referee indicates the winner, and the contestants bow first to each other and then to the joseki, and leave the area.

winning
The contestant with the higher number of total points is the winner. If both have equal scores, the contestant who scored higher as defender wins. If the scores made as defender are equal too, the contestant judged to have the better bearing and technique is declared the winner.

scoring as attacker
The target area is the chest, from the shoulders to the belt line. A scoring attack must: have correct posture, with shoulders square to front; start from the hip line; be a thrusting movement; start at least one pace away from the defender; and strike with the knife tip first.

Also the attacking arm must be fully extended at the moment it strikes, and the leg on the same side forward. An unimpeded attack scores one point.

An attack does not score if it is deflected by the defender and then hits the target area; or if it is deflected by the defender who then hits the knife because he starts an aikido technique.

scoring as defender
The defender can score with any well-carried-out aikido technique in which the attacker is thrown, made to submit, or rendered harmless. A perfect technique scores one point, one that is 80 per cent correct scores half a point. A score is also awarded if the attacker drops the knife as the result of a correct defensive technique; or if the attacker is thrown out of the area, when the defender has been within it throughout the technique.

after a score
When one of the contestants has scored the referee calls "matte," and both contestants return to their starting positions. The referee announces "ippon" or "waza-ari," and indicates the scorer. When he calls "hajime," fighting resumes. A technique scores if delivered simultaneously with the end of time.

interruptions

The referee calls ''yame'' and interrupts the fight and the timing, if a contestant:
goes out of the area;
breaks the rules;
has an accident, is injured, or becomes ill;
or needs to adjust his clothing.

He may also interrupt it for any other reason he thinks necessary. The contestants return to their starting positions, and fighting resumes when the referee calls ''hajime.''

fouls

The following are fouls: unsportsmanlike, dangerous, or over-forceful behavior or techniques;

behavior or techniques against the spirit of aikido; grasping clothing, grappling, or preventing action in any other way;

disobeying the referee, or stopping to adjust one's clothing without his permission;

and repeatedly stepping outside the competition area. It is also a foul not to use the same knife hand throughout one's round as attacker.

penalties

If they commit a foul, contestants may be warned, lose one point, or be disqualified.

If a penalty is given three times, disqualification is automatic.

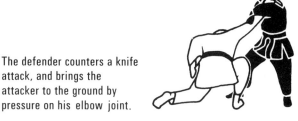

The defender blocks a knife attack from above.

The defender counters a knife attack, and brings the attacker to the ground by pressure on his elbow joint.

The defender checks a frontal attack, and counterattacks to wrist and chin, throwing the attacker backward.

A wristhold technique throws the attacker to the ground.

Ninin dori

In *ninin dori*, three participants work together in a spontaneous mock fight. Each acts as *tori* (defender) for 40 seconds.

procedure
The participants stand at the edge of the area, face joseki, and bow. The first tori takes up position in the center of the area, with joseki on his right. The two ukes (attackers) stand facing tori about 2 meters away from him. Each 40-second round begins on the call ''hajime'' and ends on ''yame.'' The uke on tori's right always begins the attack. At the end of each round, the participants return to their starting positions, and after the first and second rounds the old and new tori change places. After round three, the participants retire to the edge of the match area, hear the score for their joint performance, and bow to joseki. Rounds are interrupted if the judge calls ''yame''

rules
The ukes' attacks:
must use aikido technique;
must begin when the uke concerned is one step away from the tori;
must be positive and realistic; and must not include kicks.
Participants must stay in area.

assessment
Assessment is based on the participants' posture and techniques, their use of the area, their tactics and stamina, the number of different forms of attack and defense used, the speed of performance, and on each tori's reactions and awareness under stress. Scoring is as for kata.

For *randori kyoghi*, two unarmed contestants free-fight each other for one round. There is no set routine, and the competitors may use any aikido technique.

procedure

This is as for tanto randori, except that no knife is used, and the contest lasts for one round only. A full round lasts two minutes or more, but the fight ends if one contestant scores two full points.

scoring

As for the defender in tanto randori. Contestants must remain in the basic aikido position, and must attack with shomenate action. After a score has been made, the procedure is also as for tanto randori.

winning

The first contestant to reach two full points wins. If neither does so, the contestant with the higher number of points at the end is declared the winner. If contestants have an equal number of points, the victor is decided on bearing and technique.

interruptions and fouls

As for tanto randori.

Ate	General term for hitting techniques in karate.
Chui	A warning by the referee for a foul.
Hajime	Term used to start a contest.
Hansoko-make	Disqualification in judo.
Hansoku	Disqualification in karate.
Hansokui-chui	Public reprimand for a foul by the referee.
Hantei	The call for the final score or for a decision by the judges.
Hikkiwake	A draw in karate and aikido.
Ippon	One point.
Joseki	The chief guest at a contest.
Kachi	A victory by superiority in karate.
Kansetsu-waza	General term in judo for lock joints, which are prohibited in competition.
Judogi	Costume worn in judo.
Karate-gi	Costume worn in karate.
Karateka	Practitioner of karate.
Kata	A set formal sequence of techniques.
Katamewaza	General term for holding techniques in judo.
Kawazugaka	Foul in judo in which the contestant entwines one leg around one of his opponent's legs.
Keikoku	Penalty awarded in judo.
Keri	General term for kicking techniques in karate.
Makiwara	Striking board, used for practicing blows in karate.
Matte	Order used to interrupt a contest.
Nage	General term for throwing techniques in karate.
Nagewaza	General term for throwing techniques in judo.

Ne-waza	General term for techniques used in judo when fighting on the floor.
Ninin dori	Type of aikido contest in which the participants engage in a mock fight.
Obi	Belt worn with costume.
Randori kyoghi	Type of aikido contest in which the contestants engage in free-fighting.
Rei	The order to contestants to bow to one another.
Shiaijo	Contest area in judo.
Shido	Penalty awarded in judo.
Shobu ippon hajime	Order signaling start of karate contest.
Shomenate	Certain techniques in aikido.
Soremade	Order used to signal the end of a round or contest.
Tanto ippon	Point gained for a knife strike in *tanto randori*.
Tanto randori	Type of aikido contest in which one contestant is armed with a rubber knife.
Tori	The thrower (defender) in aikido.
Tsuki	General term for thrusting techniques in karate.
Uke	The attacker in aikido.
Uchi	General term for snapping techniques in karate.
Waza-ari	Half a point.
Waza-ari awasette ippon	A half-point that brings a competitor's score up to one point.
Yame	Order used to interrupt a contest.
Yuseigachi	Victory by superiority in judo.
Zanshin	Constant alertness of mind, one of the qualities sought in a *karateka*.

A German wood engraving of the 16th century ridicules the then outdated traditions of knightly combat.

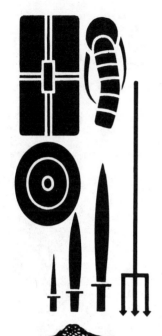

Gladiatorial combat was combat to the death –
perhaps the most brutal form of "sport" ever
known. For over three hundred years, crowds
throughout the Roman Empire flocked to see men
set to kill each other. Every sizable town had its
amphitheater for the "games." Not only did
spectators revel in this blood-letting – they had
a real part in it too. For if a gladiator was beaten
and at his adversary's mercy, the crowd would
intervene, gesturing if he was to be spared or to
die.

The gladiators were usually prisoners of war,
slaves, or condemned criminals – though sometimes freemen entered the arena, out of despera-
tion or bravado. In fact, though they only came
to a tiny minority, the rewards of success were
very great. After a gladiator had survived many
fights, he was freed, and became as wealthy and
admired as any modern pop star.

The armory and weaponry of
gladiatorial combat.

A Roman mosaic of the 4th
century A.D. depicts victory –
and death – in the arena.

Gladiators were trained in special schools, owned by the state and by wealthy citizens. There were various distinct types of gladiator – for the crowd would often spend the whole day watching the spectacle, and insisted on variety. There were set pieces between men armed in different ways – as well as between men and wild animals. One such set piece was that between secutor and retiarius. The secutor was fully armed, with helmet, shield, and sword. The retiarius wore only a short tunic, and wielded a trident; but he also had a net, in which to ensnare his opponent. Other combinations also set heavily armed men against those lightly armed but more mobile. Samnites and mirmillones, for example, had helmets, swords, and shields, while thraces fought with only shield and dagger, and dimacheri with just two short swords, one in each hand.

From earliest times, men have used mock combat as a way of training for war. And often the sport has survived for some time after its practical purpose has gone, superseded by newer methods of warfare. This process can be seen in the history of knightly combat. The medieval knight on horseback was eventually toppled by the rise of firearms and the restricting weight of his own armor – as well as by social changes. But jousting, using the armor and weaponry of knighthood, seemed to gain in popularity, even as the reality of the old chivalry was dying.

In real warfare, suits of chain mail (**a**) gave way in the 13th and 14th centuries to plate armor (**b**), made from sheets of metal. With the rise of jousting, special suits of plate armor began to be made for the purpose. Here is shown 16th-century foot combat armor from Milan (**c**) and Austria (**d**), tilting armor made for Henry VIII of England in 1540 (**e**), and German tilting armor made in 1580 (**f**).

Mock combat on horseback included tournaments between groups of cavalry, as well as jousts between individual knights. For both, sharp lances and war armor were sometimes used; but blunt lances and special jousting armor were more usual.
The horses were protected too.

Mock battles were fought at tournaments between men on foot, as well as men on horseback. Usually the opponent had to be knocked off his feet. So the weapons were as heavy as the armor: battle axes, maces, halberds, and massive two-handed swords.

In jousting on horseback, the tilt was a wooden barrier sometimes used to keep the contestants' horses from colliding.

Jousts were generally organized by a group of knights offering to challenge all comers. The aim was usually to break an opponent's lance, rather than to knock him off his horse.

Swords have been used in war and contest for thousands of years. There is an Egyptian relief from 1,200 B.C., portraying a fencing match. Yet, paradoxically, it was only with the development of firearms that skilled swordsmanship as we know it today began. Until then, in medieval times, men had fought clad in heavy armor, and weapons had to be really strong to make any impact. Once armor lost its purpose, swords grew lighter and easier to handle, and real skill in their use was essential.

Contrasting styles of swordplay from different times and places. The German two-handed sword of the 16th century (above) was clumsy in appearance, but easier to handle than it looks. It was usually held with the right hand just behind the cross-guard, and the left hand on the pommel.

The dusack, which originated in Turkey, was exclusively a cutting weapon. It demanded a good deal of agility and was difficult to parry, the best defense being counterattack.

Military traditions of swordplay were maintained by various 18th- and 19th-century weapons – such as the military broadsword shown here.

The saber, a fast cutting sword, and the bayonet, a deadly combination of sword and firearm for close-hand combat. Both came to prominence in the 19th century.

The traditional long sword of the Japanese samurai was also more of a cutting than a thrusting weapon.

In the 17th century the rapier evolved basically as a thrusting weapon – very light, with a lethal point, and little cutting edge. This established fencing movements still seen in foil and épée today.

The 17th-century stiletto (left), and the 19th-century bowie knife (right) – two weapons carried for self-defense in hand-to-hand combat.

By the 17th century, the rapier dominated European swordsmanship. With it had developed a general body of knowledge in the skills of the sword fight. Sword fighting was now an art – even a science – with recognizable patterns of move and countermove. But the long rapier was still a rather cumbersome weapon for defense; a knife was often held in the other hand, to help out at close quarters. Then, in the late 17th century, the development of the small sword transformed the situation. Here was a light, maneuverable weapon – a purely thrusting sword with no cutting edge – yet capable of meeting all the demands of real combat.

Above is a 17th-century Spanish rapier, below an 18th-century English small sword. One story of the evolution of the small sword is that it was first introduced at the court of Louis XIV, as a "toy" sword for wearing with court dress. Only later was its effectiveness realized.

Basic fighting positions from an Italian manual of the late 17th century. The cutting position, with the sword above the head, shows that the rapier is the weapon. But the on guard and lunge positions were to pass straight into small sword play, and in turn into modern fencing.

The Spanish style of sword
fighting made it into almost
a ritual dance of death. It was
as far as could be imagined
from the rough and tumble of
medieval days, when combat
had been a glorified wrestling
match that included grappling,
kicking, and using the sword
pommel as a club.

Fencing

The sport of fencing has grown naturally out of the traditions of swordsmanship. At first, fencing masters taught their art in order to prepare soldiers for battle – indeed the foil was first evolved in the 17th and 18th centuries as a practice weapon. Gradually, however, fencing became established as a sport – some would say an art – in its own right, as the dueling field was deserted for the law court, and the changing conditions of warfare demanded new military skills.

In fact, many people feel that fencing is the ideal combat sport. Fencers must use all their skills, both physical and mental, to defeat an opponent; yet theirs is not a violent sport, and mere brute force brings no advantage at all. Indeed, people of virtually any age, build, and strength can fight one another on equal terms.

At first, fencing does usually seem a very elaborate sport, with many difficult techniques to master. These, though, are an essential part of fencing. They demand mental dexterity, the ability to look ahead and to counter an opponent's move almost before he has begun it. True, they are not easy to master, and fencing lessons should always be taken from a fully qualified instructor; but once developed they will never be forgotten.

Equipment

Fencing is a very safe sport. This is chiefly because everyone who takes part, whether a beginner or a fencer with years of experience, must always wear the correct equipment, and ensure that it is kept in good condition. This means that some money has to be spent when you first start fencing (though most clubs will probably lend you equipment to begin with). But you will find it is money well spent, for equipment, so long as it is well looked after, rarely has to be replaced.

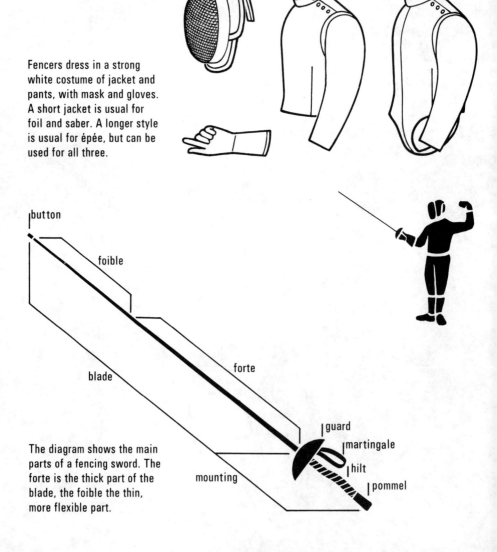

Fencers dress in a strong white costume of jacket and pants, with mask and gloves. A short jacket is usual for foil and saber. A longer style is usual for épée, but can be used for all three.

button

foible

blade

forte

guard

martingale

hilt

pommel

mounting

The diagram shows the main parts of a fencing sword. The forte is the thick part of the blade, the foible the thin, more flexible part.

Three types of sword are used in fencing: the foil, first developed as a practice sword in schools of swordsmanship; the épée, the traditional dueling sword; and the cut-and-thrust saber. At foil and épée, hits may only be scored with the point. But in saber-fencing the front edge and the third of the back edge nearest the point may also be used.

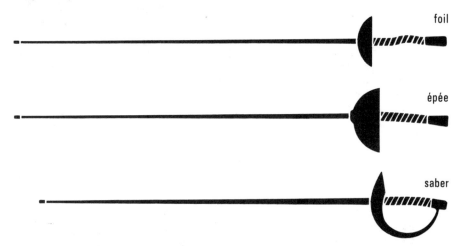

foil

épée

saber

foil

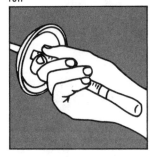

épée

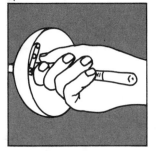

saber

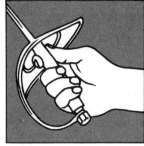

grip
Correct grip is vital, for fast sword movements are made with the fingers, not with arm or wrist. (Also, if you are left-handed, get advice on the appropriate handle and blade settings.)
foil Let the hilt rest curve down, in the palm of your hand, and grip it near the guard between your thumb and the middle of your index finger. These two fingers direct the foil's movement.

The others curl round to rest on the concave side of the hilt and press it lightly against the base of your thumb. Your wrist should be flexed slightly, so the flat of the pommel rests flat against the wrist. An orthopedic handle (with special grips) may be less tiring, but it is best not to learn with one of these.
épée The grip is as for the foil, but firmer, and may be made further from the guard to gain length. Again,

orthopedic handles are available, and can modify the grip needed.
saber This is held lightly in the fingers, not in the palm of the hand. The tips of your index finger and thumb grip the handle near the guard. The tip of your little finger presses the pommel end into the fleshy pad at the base of the little finger. The other fingers wrap lightly around the handle.

the target

At foil (**a**), the target is the trunk of the body, including the neck but not the bib of the mask.

At épée (**b**), the target is the whole of the competitor and his clothing.

At saber (**c**), the target is all the body above an imaginary line between where the tops of the thighs join the hips. It includes the arms and mask.

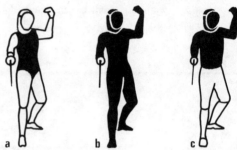

a   b   c

foil

Foil fencing is governed by rules on priority: a fencer claims priority by going into the attack, and his opponent may not counterattack until he has parried the attack. For details, see the competition rules on p. 140.

épée

In épée there is no restriction on priority. Instead, fencing is much closer to the old realities of the duel. Any hit counts, and (since the target includes the hands and arms) fencers tend to keep at a greater distance from each other.

saber

Again, the rules of priority apply, as in foil, but the difference here is that the saber is a cut-and-thrust weapon that can score with the edge as well as the point. As a result, attack and defense tactics are rather different.

fencing measure
Except when you attack, you should try to keep a set distance between yourself and your opponent. This distance, called the fencing measure, should be such that you could just touch your target with an extreme lunge forward.

on guard position
foil Your feet are at right angles, about 18 inches apart. Your weight is on both. Front foot and knee point at your opponent; your rear heel is in line behind the front foot. Your legs are bent so the knees are over the insteps. Your body is erect, sword arm side turned to the opponent – but not so far that it puts strain on the hips. Shoulders and hips are parallel. Your sword hand is chest high. Forearm and sword point slightly up, with elbow in line with body.
épée Your position is as for the foil, except that the feet are a little closer and the knees bent less, while your sword arm is more extended and points at your opponent's arm. Your elbow is tucked well in, and your wrist flexed out slightly.
saber Your position is as for the épée, except that your free hand rests in a fist on your rear hip, and your sword hand is at waist level and to the outside of the body, with elbow a little bent and the sword pointing up at your opponent's eyes.

lunge

This launches your attack. From the on guard position (**1**), stretch your sword arm straight out (**2**). (At foil and saber, this establishes your priority as attacker.) Then snap your back leg straight, sliding your front foot forward (**3**). (In foil, your rear arm comes down to just above your rear leg.) Do not move your rear foot. Keep your body erect.

return to on guard

To retreat back from a lunge (**1**) to on guard, you simultaneously bend your rear leg and push back just off the ground with your front foot (**2**). Your rear arm also starts to return to its position behind your head. Finally your sword arm returns to its bent on guard position (**3**).

reprise

This is a second attack, often used when your opponent has parried your first attack and moved back. From your lunge (**1**), you bring your back leg forward into a crouched on guard position (**2**), then lunge again (**3**).

flèche

This is a running attack, most often used at épée or saber. From on guard (**1**), you extend your sword arm and throw your body forward (**2**), bringing your rear foot off the ground. Step forward with this foot (**3**). The point of your sword should reach target just as the foot reaches the ground (**4**).

the target

The target as you see it can be divided into four, as shown. These four areas are called "lines." The high lines are those above your opponent's sword hand when he is on guard, the low ones those below. Similarly, the inside are to the open side of his sword hand, the outside to the other side.

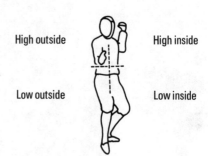

High outside

High inside

Low outside

Low inside

line of engagement

Whenever your sword is crossed with your opponent's, the relative positions of the swords mean that only part of the target is immediately open to you. For example, if your sword is outside your opponent's, and crossing it above the height of his hand, then you are only threatening the high outside line.

straight thrust

You can attack in the line of engagement with a straight thrust. This is simply the lunge already described (p. 132). But your opponent will usually be offering you very little target in this line: he will be pressing your sword away from him.

attacks on the blade

One way of dealing with the problem can be to push your opponent's blade out of the way with your own: with a quick sharp blow ("beat"), or with steady pressure as shown, But usually he will make sure to take pressure on the strong part of his blade, against the flexible part of yours.

changing the line

A better attack is usually to change the line of engagement suddenly, by moving your sword to the other side of your opponent's. Then his blade may be pressing the wrong way for a moment, and you can lunge in. Two such changes are the disengage (**a**), and the cutover (**b**). Both are semicircular movements of your blade – one under his, one over it. The disengage is made with a finger movement, the cutover by a sharp lift of the blade using fingers, wrist, and forearm.

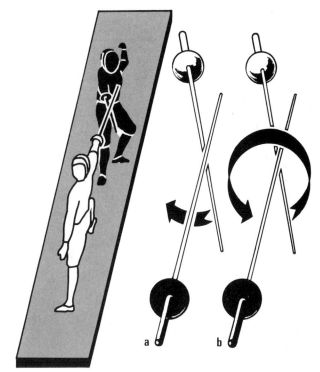

saber cuts

At saber, you can still score with the point, as in foil and épée. But you can also score a cut, with the cutting edge of the blade or with the first part of the back edge. The drawings show cuts to head (**a**) and flank (**b**). The hand has to be turned various ways, to bring the cutting edge against the target. The actual strike is a finger movement, not an arm one. Heavy hitting is slow, and painful to your opponent.

A saber cut does not count if your blade flexes across your opponent's blade, to strike him after he has parried it. But if it strikes just as he parries it, it does count.

parries

You parry an opponent's attack by deflecting his sword with your own. This works best if the strong part of your blade meets the weak part of his. There are various recognized parries, each with a French name. The basic ones are sixte, quarte, octave, and septime. Each protects a different quarter as shown.

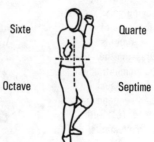

Sixte   Quarte

Octave   Septime

a   b

a   b

a   b

simple parries

Sixte and quarte are simple parries, i.e., straight movements of the sword. Sixte (**a**) takes the attacking sword outside the target, quarte (**b**) inside it. The parry can be a push (taking the other sword with it) or a strike (hitting it away). Note that the whole of the parrying sword moves, not point or hand separately.

semicircular parries

Octave (**a**) and septime (**b**) are semicircular parries, which start over the top of the attacking blade, and take it down and to one side. The action is a rotation of the wrist: the sword hand does not move down.

circular parries (counter-parries)

In these, wrist and fingers move the blade in a tight circle. They are used if your opponent tries to change the line of engagement. They pick up the attacking blade, and take it back to where it was. The drawings show the counterparries of sixte (**a**) and quarte (**b**).

saber parries

These are to protect against cuts, and so must be stronger than parries against thrusts. Tierce (**a**) and quarte (**b**) guard against horizontal cuts, quinte (**c**) against vertical cuts, and seconde (**d**) and prime (**e**) against diagonal ones.

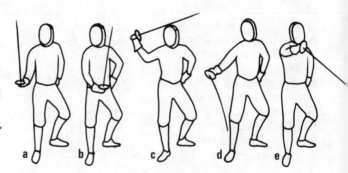
a   b   c   d   e

riposte

This is an attacking move from a successful parry. A good parry, in fact, is one that allows a good riposte. But a riposte can also be parried, and riposted in turn. The sequence shows a parry (**1**), an attempted riposte parried on the lunge (**2**), and a successful riposte by the attacker (**3**).

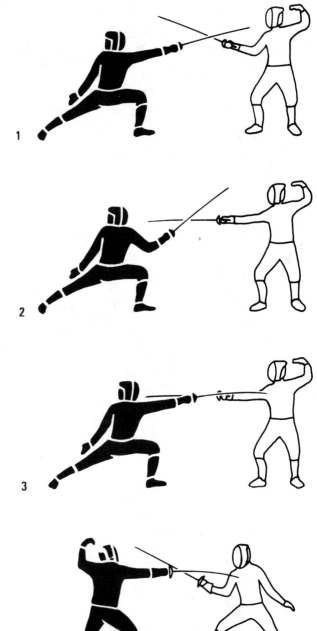

stop hit

This is used to stop an attacker in the middle of his attacking sequence. Since it scores as well as defends, it is the one exception to the rule of priority (p. 140). But it must still arrive before the attacker starts the last movement of his attack, and the same applies to stop cuts at saber. (At épée, though, stop hits can be used freely.)

Rules of fencing

The International Fencing Federation has established the recognized rules for fencing competitions.

the piste
The fencing area, which may be in or out of doors, must be flat and evenly lit. Wood, linoleum, rubber, plastic, and metallic mesh surfaces are all permitted. The piste is 2 meters wide and normally 14 meters long (13 meters is the minimum).

a center line
b on guard line
c warning line (épée and saber)
d warning line (foil)
e rear limit (all weapons)

officials
The president (**f**) is in charge of each bout. He is assisted by four judges (**g**) – or only two if electronic scoring equipment is used. The president and judges together make up the jury. Other officials include scorers, timekeepers, and electronic equipment supervisors.

events
The usual categories of competition are foil, épée, and saber for men, and foil for women. Epée and saber competitions for women are beginning to be held.

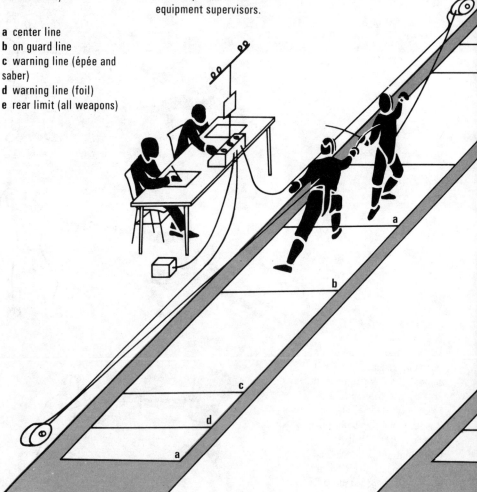

use of the piste

In all events, contestants start facing each other at the center of the piste, 4 meters apart, each contestant behind one of the guard lines (**b**). They then fight up and down along the length of the piste. But there are limits to how far a fencer may retreat from his opponent.

In foil, a fencer is warned if he retreats so that his rear foot touches or crosses the warning line (**d**). If he goes on to cross the rear limit (**e**) with both feet, a penalty hit is recorded against him. In épée and saber, a fencer who retires as far as the rear limit once is then restarted at the warning line (**c**) without immediate penalty. But if he crosses the rear limit again a penalty hit is recorded against him.

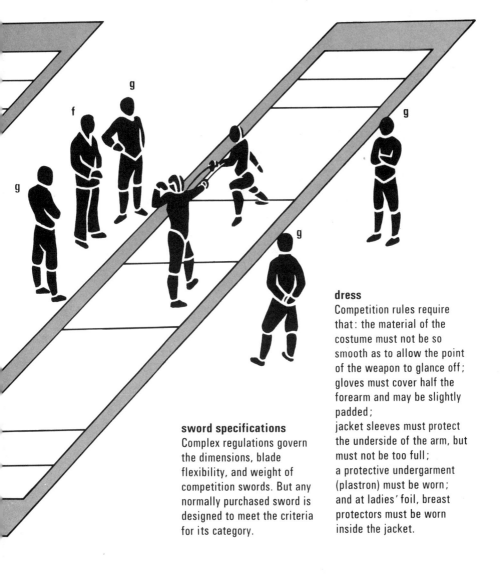

sword specifications

Complex regulations govern the dimensions, blade flexibility, and weight of competition swords. But any normally purchased sword is designed to meet the criteria for its category.

dress

Competition rules require that: the material of the costume must not be so smooth as to allow the point of the weapon to glance off; gloves must cover half the forearm and may be slightly padded; jacket sleeves must protect the underside of the arm, but must not be too full; a protective undergarment (plastron) must be worn; and at ladies' foil, breast protectors must be worn inside the jacket.

duration

The time limit for a bout is six minutes. Stoppages do not count toward the total.

winning

The winner of a bout is the first competitor to score five hits. If neither competitor scores the required number, the winner is the one leading at the time limit. If contestants have an equal score, then the bout continues until one contestant scores once more to win the bout.

procedure

The two competitors stand facing each other behind their respective on guard lines. The one first called onto the piste has his open side toward the president. The president calls ''on guard. asks the contestants if they are ready, and then calls ''play.''
Only the president may stop the bout (by calling ''halt''). After a valid hit, both contestants go back to their positions behind the on guard lines, and the bout resumes. If a hit is invalid, play continues at the spot where it halted. Hits made before ''play'' or after ''halt'' have been annulled.

scoring

To score a hit, a fencer must strike his opponent's target area with his sword point. In saber, a hit with the cutting edge, or with the third of the back edge nearest the point, also counts. (In foil and saber, hits off target count as good if the defender took up an extreme position to avoid being hit on target.) If electronic equipment is not being used, competitors change ends after one of them has scored half the required number of hits.

attack and defense

For a hit to be valid in foil or saber, the fencers' movements must follow the rule of priority. That is, when attacked a fencer must parry before he may make a riposte The attacker is whichever fencer first makes the move to threaten the target area with sword arm outstretched (**a**). He is considered to remain on the attack until his opponent has parried (**b**). So the phrase (sequence of actions) must be in the order: attack, parry, riposte, parry ,etc.
However, with a composed attack – that is, several movements made to mislead the opponent – the defender may make a stop hit at his opponent (**c**), provided his hit reaches target before the final movement of the attack has started.
In épée there is no set phrase, and no priority of movement.

a

b

c

judging hits

As soon as a judge sees a hit he raises his hand to inform the president, who then decides on the correctness of the phrase (in foil or saber), and also consults the judges and/or electronic equipment to check that a hit actually occurred. If a hit did occur and the phrase was correct, the hit is valid.

double hits

In foil and saber, if both fencers make a hit at the same time:

either both began an attack simultaneously, in which case both hits are annulled;

or, more usually, one fencer is breaking the rule of priority, and only the other fencer's hit is valid (**d**).

In épée, the scoring light is the only judge. If 1/20 of a second or more separates the hits, only the first is valid. If the hits are within 1/20 of a second of each other, a hit is recorded against both fencers.

fouls and penalties

Fighting at close quarter is allowed only if the fencers can wield their weapons correctly. Bodily contact (corps à corps) (**e**) in foil and saber is punished first by a warning, then by a penalty of one hit. In épée, bodily contact is permitted so long as there is no excessive violence. Ducking and turning are allowed, and the unarmed hand may touch the piste. If the fencers pass each other, however, the president must halt the bout and reposition the competitors. A hit made while passing is valid; one made after passing is not, unless it is an immediate riposte.

If he crosses the side limits of the piste, a fencer loses 1 meter of ground at foil, 2 meters at épée and saber. Any hit made while off the piste is invalid. If he goes over the side lines to avoid being hit, a fencer is penalized by one hit if he has already been warned. The same is imposed for crossing the rear limits after a warning.

The sword must be held in one hand. A fencer may change hands only if given permission by the president. Also, a sword may not be thrown: the hand must not leave the hilt.

The use of the free hand for either attack or defense (**f**) is prohibited. Any hit made with the help of the unarmed hand is annulled. Persistent infringement results in award of a hit to the opponent. Causing prolonged interruptions brings a penalty first of a warning, then of one hit. Dishonest or incorrect fencing, intentional brutality, vindictive actions, or refusing to obey the orders of officials, are all punished by a warning at the first offense, a penalty hit at the second, and exclusion from the competition at the third.

d

e

f

Button	The blunt end of a fencing blade.
Corps à corps	Body-to-body fighting between contestants.
Cut	A movement (or hit) with the cutting edge of a blade.
Epée	One of the three weapons used in modern fencing; based on the traditional dueling sword.
Flèche	Running attack, most often used in épée and saber.
Foible	The thinner, more flexible part of a sword's blade.
Foil	One of the three weapons used in modern fencing; evolved as a practice weapon in the 17th and 18th centuries.
Forte	The thicker, stronger part of a sword's blade.
High lines	Those parts of a fencer's body above his sword hand when he is in the on guard position.
Inside lines	Those parts of a fencer's body to the open side of his sword hand in the on guard position.
Line of engagement	The part of the target that a sword is threatening.
Low lines	Those parts of a fencer's body below his sword hand when he is in the on guard position.
Lunge	Movement used to make an attack.
Measure	Distance between two contestants when fencing.
On guard	The basic fencing position, which allows a fencer to attack or defend as necessary.
Open side	In the fencing position, the side of a fencer's body away from his sword arm.
Orthopedic handle	Any specially shaped sword handle with added grips to make control easier.

Outside lines	Those parts of a fencer's body to the blind side of his sword hand in the on guard position.
Parry	Defensive action in which the fencer deflects his opponent's sword with his own.
Phrase	Sequence of movements culminating in a hit.
Piste	Area on which a contest takes place.
Plastron	Protective undergarment worn in competitions.
Pommel	The butt end of the sword hilt.
Priority	Rules restricting counterattack in foil and saber fencing.
Pronation	Position of fencer's sword hand with fingers turned down — usually used when he is guarding the lower parts of his body.
Rassemblement	Move that takes a fencer's body and legs out of danger from an opponent's attack.
Reprise	Second attack preceded by a return to the on guard position.
Riposte	Movement made by a fencer after he has successfully parried his opponent's attack.
Saber	One of the three weapons used in modern fencing; formerly a cut-and-thrust dueling weapon, developed from a cavalry sword.
Stop hit	Successful counterattack made on an opponent during his attack.
Supination	Position of fencer's sword hand with fingers turned upward — usually used when he is guarding the upper parts of his body.

An old Japanese print depicting samurai warriors in action.

A samurai fighter reveals the
brilliance of his swordsmanship without rising from the
ground or destroying his own
composure.

Samurai with their weapons.
In combat they often carried
two swords. The long one was
mainly used, while the short
was reserved for fighting at
close quarters or in restricted
space, and for beheading a
vanquished opponent.

All the combat sports described in this book have ancient origins. Those from the East in particular have come out of a long martial tradition. In Japan this tradition was summed up in the samurai – a caste of military fighters, already established in the 13th century, and active well into the 19th. They were skilled and dedicated warriors who lived plainly, often in great poverty, devoting their whole lives to attaining perfection in the use of the sword. For them, this dedication was part of a strict code of ethics, and of the philosophy of *bushido*, the "way of the warrior" – an idea rather like the European concept of knightly chivalry.

Kendo

Kendo means "sword way," and is the Japanese name for the art of sword fighting. Like other oriental martial sports, it is rooted in history. Like them, it makes great physical demands, and requires considerable self-discipline. And like them, too, it allows women to compete on equal terms with men.

Kendo has its origins in samurai tradition. There are references as early as 400 A.D. to weapon practice using wooden swords. Throughout medieval times in Japan such skills were very relevant, and were kept alive in countless warrior schools. With the decline of the samurai in the 19th century, kendo too declined, although it was already more sport than battle training. But in the present century, like the other martial arts, it has greatly revived.

Kendo today is a very safe sport. The "swords" used are of bamboo, and special garments protect the body. It is also a very ritualistic sport; kendoists even wear the traditional dress of the samurai era. Nevertheless, it still has many features that belong to its very practical origins. The target areas are those most relevant in a real fight with samurai swords. Similarly, the cuts and thrusts judged good in a contest are those that would be needed to deal with a real opponent. Also, despite the ritual of kendo, there is perhaps less emphasis than in other oriental martial sports on formal grading, and more on real fighting ability.

dress

To practice or compete at kendo, you wear:
a a shirt, ankle-length baggy pants, and a toweling headcloth;
b a mask (men in Japanese);
c a breastplate (do);
d a protective apron (tare); and
e gauntlets (kote).

shinai

The shinai, or sword, (**f**) has a blade made of four staves of bamboo. Each one of these runs the full length of the shinai. They are held together by the leather hilt; by a small leather cup at the point; by a leather strip that binds around the staves halfway along; and by a cord that runs from hilt to cup. A circular piece of leather around the hilt acts as a guard. The shinai is a little under 4 feet long, and weighs about a pound.

a   b   c   d   e   f

preliminary ritual

A practice bout at kendo begins with a set ritual. The contestants stand six paces apart, bow (**1**), and crouch (**2**). Each draws his shinai, and holds it pointing at his opponent's head (**3**), so the tips of the shinai just cross. Then both contestants rise into the fighting position (**4**), with shinai tips still crossed.

sword grip

The shinai is gripped with the left hand firmly on the butt end of the hilt, and the right hand just behind the guard. The shinai is swung from the shoulders in broad, circular movements.

basic stance

The feet point forward, with the heels slightly raised. The right foot is in front, but weight is equal on both. Movement is by gliding steps, just off the floor. The basic shinai position is pointing at the opponent's head, as in (**4**) below.

1   2   3   4

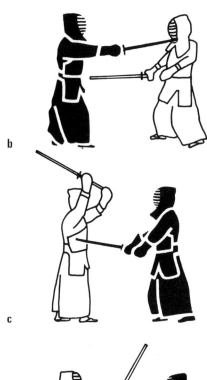

The targets for blows are:
a the top and the left and right temples of the headmask (men);

b the throat protector (tsuki);

c the left and right breast-plates (do); and

d the right wrist, and also the left wrist if the left hand is at shoulder height or higher (kote). Blows to all these must be cuts, except for blows to the throat when a thrust must be used. Thrusts are scored with the point of the shinai. Cuts are scored with the third of the shinai blade nearest the point. Also the string running from hilt to point is used to represent the back of the sword; so cuts must use the opposite edge to this.

For a blow to score in a contest, it must be made with style and vigor, and the scorer should shout as he strikes. The Japanese names are given to the targets. The words hidari (left) and migi (right) are used to make this more precise. So "hidari men," for example, means a blow to the left temple. ("O-shomen" is used to indicate a blow to the top of the head.)

Rules of kendo

The first kendo world championships were held in Japan in 1970. Afterward, the International Kendo Federation was established, and its rules now apply in all major competitions.

officials

These include:
a the judge-in-chief, who sits outside the competition area;
b the chief referee, who is inside the competition area;
c two assistant referees, also in the area;
d two line judges;
e a timekeeper and assistant(s);
f a scorekeeper and assistant(s).

The judge-in-chief has the final decision if the other judges disagree. (In his absence, he is represented by a judge-in-charge.) The three judges inside the area control conduct, point out and rule on valid techniques and on infringements, and decide the victor if necessary. They each have an allotted line of vision, and use red and white flags to signal with.

area

Contests take place on a smooth wooden-floored rectangular area, usually 10 meters by 11 meters. It is marked with boundary lines, a center cross or circle, and two starting lines. There must be a clear space at least 1·5 meters wide around the boundary of the competition area.

shinai

If one shinai is used, it must be under 118 centimeters long, and weigh at least 485 grams. For those bouts in which a contestant has two shinai, the longer shinai must be no more than 110 centimeters long, and must weigh over 375 grams, while the shorter must have a maximum length of 60 centimeters and a minumum weight of 265 grams.

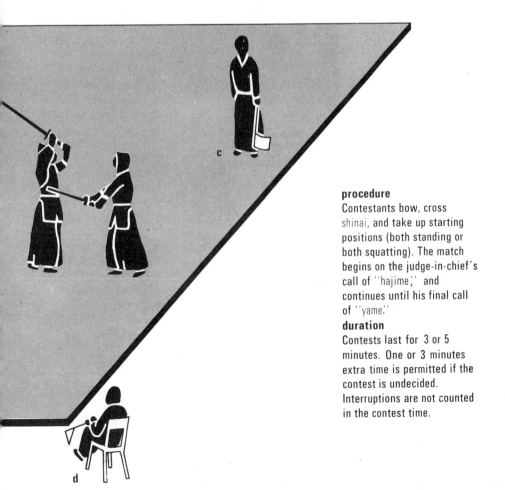

procedure

Contestants bow, cross shinai, and take up starting positions (both standing or both squatting). The match begins on the judge-in-chief's call of "hajime," and continues until his final call of "yame."

duration

Contests last for 3 or 5 minutes. One or 3 minutes extra time is permitted if the contest is undecided. Interruptions are not counted in the contest time.

scoring

The scoring blows are given on p. 151. One point is awarded for a blow delivered with full spirit and correct form. One judge's vote is sufficient if the other judges are undecided.

Blows still count even if they are delivered as the opponent drops his shinai, or steps or falls out of the area, or as time is called.

result

The winner is the first contestant to score two points, or the one with the higher score at the end of time. If the contestants are equal at the end of time, the judges may declare a draw, or award victory to one of the contestants, or allow extra time. In extra time, the contestant who scores first wins.

separating contestants

Contestants are separated: if one fall or drops his shinai and his opponent does not immediately strike an effective blow (the restart is at the starting lines); or if the contestants are in a prolonged hilt-to-hilt with no apparent intention of striking a blow (the restart is at the same point).

signals

Signals used by the judges in the competition area are:
a effective cut or thrust – flag raised diagonally upward in the direction of the scorer;
b no effective blow – both flags waved downward in front of body;
c cannot judge – both flags crossed downward in front of body, red flag out;
e separate contestants when they are hilt to hilt – both flags extended forward at shoulder height and parallel to one another.
d interrupt the match – both flags raised;

announcements

The following announcements may be made:
men ari (or kote, do, or tsuki ari) – successful scoring technique on the part of the body named (see p. 151);
yame – interruption;
nikonme – restart after one point has been scored;
shobu – restart after one point has been scored by each contestant;
encho hajime – restart for extra time;
shobu ari – a victory and the end of the match;
hikiwake – a draw.

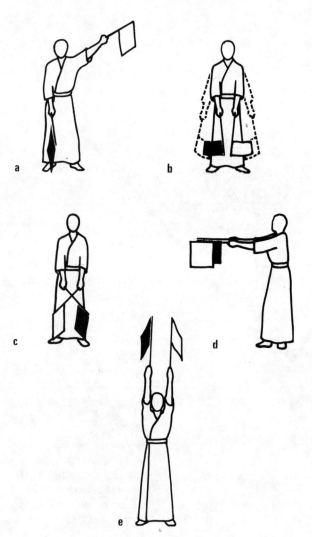

fouls

A competitor may not:
a illegally shove or thrust with his shinai;
b strike at his opponent's unprotected parts;
c grasp his opponent with his hands;
d grasp his opponent's shinai above the hilt after dropping his own shinai;
use the hilt of his shinai to break his opponent's grasp on his shinai hilt;
place his foot outside the match area;
fall with any part of his body outside the match area;
use his shinai as a prop to prevent his body going outside the area;
trip his opponent;
or use or commit disrespectful or undignified words or acts.

penalties

A foul results in a caution. If the contestant fouls three times, one point is awarded to his opponent.
But disrespectful, undignified or violent acts or words are penalized by immediate disqualification.

injuries

If a contestant cannot continue because of injuries, the match is ended.
If his opponent caused the injuries, the injured man wins, with one point. If not, the injured man forfeits the match, and his opponent is awarded two points.
If a contestant asks for the match to be halted or ended, without sufficient reason, he forfeits the match, and his opponent receives two points.

a

b

c

d

Do	Breastplate worn by kendo contestants.
Do ari	Successful score on breastplate in kendo.
Encho hajime	Term used to restart kendo contest when going into extra time.
Hajime	Term used to start a kendo contest.
Hakama	Pants worn by kendo contestants.
Hidari	Left – used to indicate that a blow was on the left side of the mask or breastplate, or on the left gauntlet.
Hikiwake	Term used to announce a draw in a kendo contest.
Keikogi	Shirt worn by kendo contestants.
Kendoka	Practitioner of kendo.
Kote	Gauntlets worn by kendo contestants.
Kote ari	Successful score on the gauntlets in kendo.
Men	Mask worn by kendo contestants.
Men ari	Successful score on mask in kendo.
Migi	Right – used to indicate that a blow was on the right side of the mask or breastplate, or on the right gauntlet.
Nikonme	Term used to restart kendo contest after one point has been scored.
O-shomen ari	Successful score on the center of the mask in kendo.
Shinai	Bamboo sword used in kendo.
Shobu	Term used to restart kendo contest after one point has been scored by each contestant.
Shobu ari	Term used to announce victor at end of a kendo contest.
Tare	Protective apron worn by kendo contestants.
Tenegui	Headcloth worn by kendo contestants.
Tsuki ari	Successful score to the throat in kendo.
Yame	Term used to interrupt kendo contest.

Index